CORNELSEN SENIOR ENGLISH LIBRARY

JAMES HENEGHAN

Torn Away

Cornelsen

James Heneghan
Torn Away

Herausgegeben von
Alexandra Fest, Mechthild Hesse

Verlagsredaktion: Neil Porter

Herausgeber der Cornelsen Senior English Library:
Prof. Dr. Albert-Reiner Glaap

Umschlaggestaltung:
Cornelsen Schulverlage Design; Bildrecherche: Josephine Wolff
Umschlagfoto: Landschaft: © Phil Emmerson / Shutterstock.com;
Belfast Wandbild: © Brendan Howard / Shutterstock.com;
Mauerdurchblick: © Valzan / Shutterstock.com

Technische Umsetzung: Peter Richter

www.cornelsen.de

1. Auflage, 9. Druck 2015

Alle Drucke dieser Auflage sind inhaltlich unverändert und können
im Unterricht nebeneinander verwendet werden.

Druck: Offizin Andersen Nexö Leipzig

ISBN 978-3-464-06825-0

Inhalt gedruckt auf säurefreiem Papier aus nachhaltiger Forstwirtschaft.

CONTENTS

In memory of my mother and father

Abbreviations

adj	adjective
BE	British English
derog.	derogatory
e.g.	exempli gratia; for example
esp.	especially
etc.	et cetera; and so on
fml	formal
i.e.	id est; in other words
infml	informal
IrE	Irish English
jdn.	jemanden
NAmE	North American English
n	noun
sb.	somebody
sl	slang
sth.	something
usu.	usually
v	verb

ONE

They handcuffed him to the seat so he could cause no trouble on the airplane.

He was small for his thirteen years, and wiry, with straight brown hair worn in a fringe across a wide brow. He needed a haircut. His eyes too were brown, brooding and dark in a pale face that would have been hard were it not for the lips, which were full and soft. He wore old blue jeans, white cotton socks, worn-out sneakers, a blue cotton T-shirt, and an old grey wool sweater. He wore no watch, but on the middle finger of his left hand he had a gold wedding ring that had been his mother's.

He had the seat to himself at the back. He pressed his face up against the window, and when he saw the two plainclothes policemen disappear into the terminal, he folded his thin hand together like a Chinese fan and wriggled it out of the handcuff.

When they had dragged him aboard, everyone had stared. Now, with their heads turned to the front, they were trying to pretend he was not there. The flight attendant was standing at the open door speaking into her telephone. He would have to be quick.

He slid from his seat, took a deep breath, and hurled himself down the aisle.

▷ **1** *handcuff sb.* (v): jdm. Handschellen anlegen **3** *wiry* ['waɪəri]: small and thin, yet strong **4** *fringe* (BE): hair hanging over the forehead **5** *brooding:* dark or threatening **7** *sneakers* (infml): sports shoes **12** *plainclothes:* not in uniform **14** *fan:* Fächer · *wriggle sth.:* twist sth. quickly back and forth **15** *drag sb.:* pull sb. with force **16** *pretend:* act as if **17** *flight attendant:* Flugbegleiter/in **20** *hurl sb.* [hɜːl]: throw sb. violently **21** *aisle* [aɪl]: narrow passage between seats

Somebody shouted, "Look out!"

But he was too fast for them. He was past the flight attendant and out the door before anyone could stop him.

"Stop him!" cried the flight attendant to the uniformed boarding-pass attendant, a tall, thin man down on the tarmac.

He skipped lightly down the steps. Boarding passes fluttered to the ground as the attendant reached out to grab him, but the boy was too quick. He swerved and ducked under the man's arms and was away across the tarmac, arms pumping, legs flashing.

The flight attendant with the telephone must have alerted the check-in staff, for three women and two men were scrambling from behind their counters to form a barrier as he burst into the terminal.

He stopped to consider, his chest heaving.

They advanced on him, arms outstretched.

He turned and plunged back out the door, around the edge of the building and across the road toward the parking lot.

The man in the Avis-rental blue Vauxhall saw him run in front of the car and jumped hard on the brakes.

The boy struck the hood of the car with the palm of his hand as he went down. He lay there, still, listening.

The driver, a stout middle-aged man, scrambled out of the car in a panic. As he bent over the crumpled body, the boy leaped to his feet and kicked him hard under the jaw. The man reeled backward and lay gasping on his back. The boy jumped behind the wheel, slammed the car door shut, restarted the engine, pushed his foot down hard on the accelerator, and screeched away from the terminal.

A police car was waiting for him at the highway, blocking the way ahead. The boy jerked at the wheel desperately, pulling the car around too fast with a scream of burning rubber, and raced back toward the parking lot with the police car on his tail, siren wailing.

He rocketed through the parking lot, up one aisle, turning tightly down the other, tight turn, up the next aisle, tires screaming. The police car tried to cut him off at an exit, but the Vauxhall crashed into its fender and kept going, weaving wildly. There were two men in the car. They cut him off at the next exit, and this time when the Vauxhall collided, it came to a stop, its front bumper and grille locked in the twisted metal of the police car.

They had him.

They were angry. They wrestled him to the terminal and locked him in the baggage room. He unzipped and ripped open as many bags and suitcases as he could and hurled their contents around the room, and when the original policemen, the ones who had put him on the airplane, got there, the place looked like a cyclone had hit a clothing store.

The flight had been delayed thirty-two minutes.

This time they took no chances. One policeman was to go with him all the way to London. He was handcuffed to the seat again, but this time the steel bit into his wrist and he could not slip his hand out. He sat on the inside, by the window. The policeman was a large, sandy, silent man who chewed gum and read the *Belfast Telegraph*.

The airplane taxied to the runway and stopped. The boy jerked at the handcuff with his free hand, but the arm of the seat was unyielding; the steel stabbed his flesh, and he bit his lip with the pain of it. The policeman did not look up from his newspaper.

It had taken them more than two months to catch him. At first they used to come to the house, knocking on the door for him to let them in. Then later, after he had joined the Holy Terrors, they came and forced the door open, and he ran out the back and down the alley. By the time they took to surrounding the house, he was no longer there but was hiding with one of the gang members.

Sometimes he hid right under their noses at the O'Malley house next door. From there he watched the police coming and going, and when their backs were turned, he was often able to sneak into his own house and sleep in his own bed.

Mr. O'Malley had tried reasoning with him. "You can't run forever, Declan. They're bound to catch you. Where will you go when they discover you here?" Mr. O'Malley wore a black patch. He had lost an

▷ **5** *tarmac:* runway **8** *swerve* [swɜːv]: change direction suddenly **10** *alert sb.:* warn sb. **11** *scramble:* move quickly **13** *heave:* rise and fall regularly **15** *plunge:* move suddenly forwards and/or downwards **17** *Vauxhall:* type of car **19** *hood:* Motorhaube **22** *leap:* jump **23** *jaw:* Kiefer · *reel:* move unsteadily **24** *gasp* (v): breathe very quickly · *slam sth.:* shut sth. forcefully and noisily **26** *accelerator:* Gaspedal · *screech away:* move with a long, harsh sound **28** *jerk:* give a quick and sudden pull · *desperate:* ready to do anything regardless of danger **30** *wail:* make a loud, shrill sound **34** *fender* (NAmE): Kotflügel · *weave:* move in a zigzag course **36** *bumper:* Stoßstange **43** *cyclone:* tornado **50** *sandy:* with yellow-red hair **53** *unyielding:* firm, fixed in place · *stab sth.:* cut into sth. **63** *sneak:* walk very softly in order not to be heard or seen **67** *patch:* piece of cloth worn over one eye

eye ten years ago to a British plastic bullet in the riots following the deaths of jailed hunger-strikers. And ten years before that, he had been thrown into the Maze prison with several hundred other Catholics, where he was kept for three years without a trial. His nerves were wrecked. He couldn't lift a cup of tea without spilling it.

Declan's friend Tim O'Malley, his face pale and worried, said, "Listen to my da, Declan, he's right. Don't I wish it was myself who was getting out of this dung heap and going off to Canada? It's lucky you are that your uncle sends for you. I hear everyone in Canada is rich."

"I was born and raised in Belfast and here I'll stay," said Declan, "and no man has the right, uncle or not, to make me go."

Tim's father said, "Your Uncle Matthew is all you have left, Declan. He has a right to claim you. He wants you. You must go."

"I won't go."

Tim's mother was very unhappy. She said, "My cousin Julia lives in New York and she loves it. Canada is close to New York and it sounds like the wonderful country, so it does. The good Lord in all his mercy will take care of you, Declan, and our prayers will go with you."

Declan said, "The good Lord is it! And prayers is it! Don't be telling me about the mercy of the good Lord, Mrs. O'Malley, haven't I had enough of it?"

Mr. O'Malley said, "Your uncle ..."

"Uncle! Matthew Doyle ran away from his country and left it to the English. He's no uncle of mine!"

Tim's mother started weeping.

"You can cry all you want, Mrs. O'Malley," said Declan, "but I'll not run from Ireland and leave the murderers go free who killed my family. If they make me go, then I'll come back."

"I'll be back," he whispered to himself now as the plane started its race, gathering speed down the runway. He pressed his cheek to the window. "I'll be back," he said again.

The plane lifted off. The boy looked down. Identical rows of livid red rooftops slid underneath the airplane, row after row of them. In the grey gloom, they looked like long angry scars on the blighted landscape.

If the policeman had not been reading his newspaper, and if he had searched the reflection in the tiny window, he might have noticed that the boy was crying.

TWO

The policeman, still chewing gum, handed Declan over to an immigration officer at London's Heathrow airport. He removed the handcuffs. "Good luck, Doyle," was all he said to the boy before he left to board the next flight back to Belfast.

"Get stuffed!" said Declan.

The immigration man's name pin said C. D. SANFORD. The man was wide and bald. He took the boy to a small room that had a desk and two chairs. "Sit down, Declan," he said in a soft voice.

Declan kicked the chair over and pushed his hands into his pockets. The chair was made of metal tubing and it made a loud clatter as it hit the floor.

The immigration man shrugged his shoulders and started to fill out a form, copying down information from the papers given to him by the police. "They have your name spelled two different ways on these papers, Declan. Is it D-E-C or D-E-K?"

The boy did not answer.

"I'll put down D-E-C, the same as your passport."

"I have no passport."

Sanford smiled. "You have now, Declan. The Belfast police rushed one through for you."

▷ **4** *trial:* Gerichtsverfahren **7** *da* (infml): father **8** *dung heap* (sl): pile of animal waste **35** *scar:* mark left by a wound after healing **35–36** *blighted landscape:* zerklüftete Landschaft **44** *get stuffed* (BE sl): used to express contempt, rejection, etc. **46** *bald* [bɔːld]: having no hair on one's head **50** *clatter* (n): rattling sound (like keys or dishes) **51** *shrug one's shoulders:* raise one's shoulders to show that one doesn't care

"And my name is pronounced DEK-lin!"

"Sorry, Declan," said Sanford, pronouncing it properly. He smiled apologetically. "I'm not so good on Irish names."

Declan went to the door and tried opening it. It was locked.

When Sanford had finished writing on his forms, he said, "Would you sign your name here for me, Declan, please?"

"Why?"

"Just look the information over, and sign that it's correct. It's only a formality." He pushed the pen and paper over the desk toward the boy.

Declan wrote on the paper, *Tiocfaidh ár iá*.

"Gaelic, Declan? What does it mean?"

"'Our day will come.' That's what it means, Mister English Immigration Officer. Wouldn't an Irishman be the fool to sign an English paper? If it wasn't for the hundreds of years of English rule there'd never be the troubles in Ireland. You English have a lot to answer for, and that's the truth."

The immigration officer gave a resigned sigh and wrote something above Declan's slogan. Then he handcuffed Declan, a different pair this time, black ones, and took him to a special detention room in the airport terminal that had in it only a bed, a chair, a small table, and behind a screen, a toilet and washbasin. Except for a tiny glass square in the door, there was no window.

"You will be kept here for the night, Declan, and early tomorrow morning we will be on a flight for Vancouver, Canada. Food will be brought to you here in your room." His smile was friendly. "Any questions?"

"We? Will you be coming with me, Seedy?"

Sanford removed the handcuffs. "I'm afraid so, Declan. You're classified as 'dangerous.' We can't take any chances until we hand you over to your uncle in Vancouver."

"I'm dangerous, all right. That's why they call me Dangerous Declan Doyle."

Sanford smiled. "Good night, Declan."

"You can stuff your good night up your snotty English nose."

He heard the key rattle in the lock, and threw himself on the bed and lay on his back, staring at the ceiling.

A man's face, not Sanford's, spied at him through the tiny window every ten minutes.

Some time later, a woman brought food on a tray while Spyface stood by the door. Declan sat on the edge of his bed and took the tray onto his lap. He picked up the soup spoon. He measured the distance to the door out of the corner of his eye. Then he slowly, carefully, took the bowl of thick, hot soup in the fingers of his left hand and with a quick flick of his wrist sent it flying like a Frisbee at Spyface at the door. The bowl hit him in the chest. Green pea soup spattered onto his face.

Declan leaped toward the door, hurling the tray with its dinner plate of meat, potatoes, and gravy at the guard as he moved. This time his aim was not quite so good, for the tray took Spyface in the knee, toppling him to the floor, but not preventing him from reaching out and getting a grip on Declan's leg as the boy tried to rush by. Declan was halfway out the door, dragging his imprisoned leg and elbowing Spyface in the head to make him let go, but the guard was too big and strong for him. He pulled Declan down to the floor and dealt him a vicious blow to the stomach that made the boy gasp with pain. Then he threw Declan onto the bed and stood over him while the woman picked up the tray and the broken dishes.

The guard was breathing heavily. "You young bastard!" he said.

Then they left. They brought no more food.

Declan had his usual nightmare, the one with the bomb exploding, waking in the early hours of the morning in terror, drenched in sweat and tears, yelling out, not knowing where he was. The guard – not Spyface, a new one – switched on the light from outside the cell and peered in. He left the light on until he saw the boy pull the covers up over himself and then he switched it off.

▷ **3** *apologetic* [ə,pɒlə'dʒetɪk]: showing that one is sorry **18** *sigh* (n): long, deep breath that can be heard **20** *detention room:* room in which a person is kept and not allowed to leave **35** *snotty:* dirty **42** *lap:* Schoß **45** *flick* (n): quick movement **46** *spatter:* splash **49** *gravy:* Bratensoße **51** *topple sb.:* cause sb. to fall **56** *vicious:* nasty; severe, violent **62** *drenched:* completely wet **65** *peer:* look carefully

THREE

The next morning, two men he had not seen before brought him a breakfast of cereal, poached eggs, toast, and orange juice. Declan was sitting bent over on the edge of his bed. He was hungry. His stomach hurt from the blow the night before. One man stood at the door while the other put the tray down on the small table. Declan lashed out with his feet, kicking over the table and sending the tray and its contents crashing to the floor. The first man reached for him but slipped on the eggs and juice and tumbled against the bed. Declan tried to duck under the second man's arms but the man, too quick and strong for him, threw him back into the room. The two men backed carefully out of the room and locked the door.

A short time later, Sanford brought him a bag of clothing. The guard stood behind him at the door. Declan looked in the bag. "I don't need your cold English charity," he said, throwing the bag back into his face. Sanford caught it quickly. He looked around at the mess of food on the floor. "You're not being sensible, Declan. How do you expect to keep up your strength if you don't eat?"

Sanford walked him aboard the airplane. He obviously knew about Declan's earlier escape, for the steel bracelet was tight on his wrist. Unlike the Irish policeman, however, the immigration officer kept his handcuffed hand hidden under his flowing raincoat.

As soon as they set foot on the 747, Declan began to protest in a voice loud enough for everyone to hear. "Why do you have to have the handcuffs so tight, Seedy? My wrist is bleeding!" And he pulled his hand from Sanford's pocket so all could see the cruelty done to a mere boy.

Heads turned. Men scowled; women's eyes and lips rounded in horror. Declan grinned at Sanford's discomfort.

They sat at the back near the washroom, the boy on the inside window seat. Sanford keyed his own cuff open and the ratchet stuttered as he locked it on the armrest so that Declan now had his left hand locked to the seat; his right was free.

"I need to go to the bathroom."

Sanford unlocked the wrist cuff and stood to let him out, blocking the escape aisle, and then followed Declan along to the washroom. "Don't lock the door."

But he did lock the door. He ran the water in the sink until it overflowed; then he blocked the toilet with paper towels and flushed and flushed until the water ran over the floor and out under the door.

Sanford forced the catch off the door, but as he crashed in and fell up against the sink, Declan squeezed past him out the door and up the aisle, only to slither and slip in the river of water coursing along the floor. He almost made it out the emergency exit, but Sanford dropped him in a swift tackle and dragged him back and handcuffed him to his seat. Declan's bruised stomach ached more than ever.

The Boeing and its 465 passengers were delayed for twenty minutes while the maintenance crew came aboard and cleaned up.

Declan watched out the window as the airplane arrowed up into the English sky. By the time they were flying over the northwest coast of Scotland and leaving the British Isles, they were six miles high.

The flight attendant came around with drinks. Declan took an orange juice.

He found it hard to believe he was leaving his native land. Ripped away from his roots. Kidnapped.

If only he could somehow turn the airplane around and go home. Impossible. Hijack the plane. Also impossible. He was helpless.

So that he could cause no trouble during the flight, the wily immigration officer had arranged for Declan's orange juice to be doctored with thioridazine, a tasteless, odorless tranquilizer often

▷ **2** *poached egg:* pochiertes/verlorenes Ei **8** *tumble:* fall **14** *charity:* generosity, kindness **19** *bracelet:* Armband **27** *scowl* (v): look angrily **30** *ratchet:* Sperrklinke **31** *stutter* (v): (here) make a repetitive sound **42** *slither:* slide or slip on a wet or frozen surface **44** *swift:* quick · *tackle* (n): act of taking hold of sb. **57** *wily:* clever in deceiving people **59** *odorless* (AE) = (BE) *odourless:* not smelling of anything

used on unwilling deportees. Declan had spilled the breakfast juice and the drug was wasted. But now the juice given him by the flight attendant was beginning to take effect.

A deep depression settled on the drugged boy. His limbs felt heavy; he slumped in his seat and closed his eyes with leaden hopelessness. He was tired. He could fight no more. He was an animal caught in a trap.

Twelve hours and thirteen minutes later, the giant 747 touched down at the Vancouver International Airport in Canada, where the time was only a little past noon the same day, Saturday, September 12. He had flown backward in time. A light rain was falling.

Sanford took him straight into the immigration office, where his uncle was waiting for him. Sanford asked the Canadian immigration officer, a dark, stocky man named Raghavji, to lock the door before he removed the handcuffs. Raghavji locked the door and introduced Sanford: "This is Mr. Matthew Doyle."

Matthew Doyle stood up and nodded at the English immigration officer without looking at him. His eyes had not left his nephew since the boy had walked into the room.

Declan, still bleary from the thioridazine, rubbed his swollen wrist where the handcuff had left blue welts and looked coldly up at his father's brother. The man he saw before him looked nothing like the young man he had seen in photographs taken in Ireland before he left for Canada. His uncle had the same brown hair and dark eyes of Declan's da, but there the resemblance ended.

Matthew Doyle was a big man, lean and spare and tall, with wide shoulders and long arms that dangled almost to his knees. The first thing Declan noticed about him, however, was not his bigness, but his sadness. Matthew Doyle had the longest, saddest face he had ever seen. He reminded Declan of one of those ugly, sorrowful dogs – he couldn't remember the kind – with the suffering eyes and woeful expression. His hands were big and gnarled, with spatulate, half-moon nails, and he wore brown cords, brown boots, a green cotton shirt, and a stained car coat that might have been beige. He looked like an odd-job man, which is what he was.

He stared at Declan with his big sad face, not saying anything.

Declan stared back at him.

When the silence became so long that the two immigration officers had decided that neither the boy nor his uncle was about to speak,

Sanford pushed a sheaf of papers across the desk and said, "Declan is now in your custody, Mr. Doyle. Please sign at the places I've marked with an X."

Matthew Doyle bent to sign the papers. Declan watched him. His uncle wrote his name and Sanford tore off a copy and gave it to him along with Declan's passport. Raghavji unlocked the door.

"Good-bye, Declan," said Sanford, "and good luck."

Declan made no reply.

"Good-bye, Mr. Doyle," said Raghavji. "Good-bye, Declan."

Matthew Doyle nodded his big head and without looking around at the boy, said, "Follow me."

Declan stumbled after him.

They walked out of the airport terminal and across the parking lot in the soft September rain.

▷ **4** *limb:* leg or arm **5** *leaden* ['ledn]: extremely heavy **7** *trap:* instrument for catching animals **14** *stocky:* stämmig **20** *bleary* ['blɪəri]: sleepy **21** *welt:* mark left on the skin **26** *lean and spare:* thin **27** *dangle:* hang down loosely **31** *woeful:* very sad **32** *gnarled:* knorrig **35** *odd-job man:* person paid to do small jobs of various types for other people **41** *custody:* right or duty to take care of sb./sth.

FOUR

If Tim O'Malley was right – that Canadians were rich – then Matthew Doyle must be the only exception, thought Declan, for in the hundreds of late-model cars in the airport parking lot, the 1962 Ford truck stood out like a dinosaur.

Matthew started the ancient motor with the gearshift in neutral and the truck shuddered to life. It seemed to Declan that his uncle leaned an ear toward whatever it was the engine was trying to tell him. After a few seconds, apparently satisfied, he stopped listening and reached across Declan and pulled open the glove compartment, from which he took a roll of mints. He held the roll out to Declan. "Mint?"

Declan tried to shake his head but the effort was too much for him. He sat in a collapsed silence.

Matthew took one for himself and tossed the roll onto the dash, where it joined a mess of pens, string, coins, and faded yellow-and-blue parking violation tickets.

His uncle persuaded the gearshift into reverse, backed the truck out of the slot, and they were soon on the road, with the Ford engine singing a sad requiem all the way to the city of Vancouver. The only windscreen wiper that worked was Matthew's, which did not bother Declan, for he was not interested in the journey anyway.

The truck rattled over the Lions Gate Bridge into West Vancouver and onto the Upper Levels Highway. Declan looked down at Howe Sound, gloomy and pensive in the mist and rain. "You don't live in Vancouver, then?"

Matthew shook his head and pointed up ahead.

Declan looked and saw nothing but the narrow mountain highway and sheer rocky walls. "You live in a cave in the rocks?" he said sarcastically.

"Otter Harbour," said Matthew.

His uncle was no great talker.

The rain stopped. The sky brightened. Horseshoe Bay was high mountains and mists, and ferryboats huge as ocean liners. He wanted to ask his uncle if they were waiting to board one of the towering ferryboats, but as soon as he thought of the question he forgot it. Ten minutes later they boarded, not one of the big ships but a very ordinary little ferry. His uncle switched off the engine and they sat in the truck with the windows rolled down as the ferry chugged out of the bay.

Matthew pointed a finger and spoke his sixth word. "Eagle," he said.

Declan watched the eagle, forcing his eyes to focus. He had never seen an eagle before, only on TV. It circled slowly over the hills. Declan could not take his eyes off it. Such freedom! To fly so high and swoop and glide in the streets of silent air!

The ferry landed at a place called Langdale, and away they drove again along a winding country road in a journey that it seemed must go on forever. Declan was reminded of a place he had read about at school, a place that was all mountains and mists and magic, that was lost in the shadows of time. It was called Shangri-la, he remembered. But that was only in a book. Besides, this place was not really like Shangri-la; if it were, he would feel happy, and he felt awful.

"Won't be long now," said Matthew.

Declan said nothing, but kept his eyes to the front, staring straight ahead; he did not care how long it took, it was all the same to him. Two could play at the game of silence.

School.

There was a time when he had liked school – he had enjoyed history, especially Irish history, with its brave stories of Ireland's

▷ **5** *ancient:* very old · *gearshift* (AE) = (BE) *gear lever:* Schaltknüppel **8** *apparently:* as it seems · *satisfied:* contented **9** *glove compartment:* Handschuhfach **13** *toss sth.:* throw sth. · *dash* (= *dashboard*): Armaturenbrett **17** *slot:* Parkbucht **23** *gloomy:* dark · *pensive:* thoughtful, worried **27** *cave:* space within a hill or underground **39** *eagle:* Adler **44** *swoop:* come down suddenly

heroes and patriots – but he had stopped going there after … after the bomb.

He had joined Brendan Fogarty's gang instead. None of them went to school. Brendan, sixteen, was the oldest. At eleven, Kevin Payne was the youngest. The Holy Terrors. Their number varied between seven and ten members, depending on whether the school inspector or the police managed to catch some of them and force them back to school for awhile.

Rebels with a cause, that was the Holy Terrors.

The way Brendan Fogarty explained it was this: "In the north of Ireland it's a war between them and us, between the Brits – the English – and the Catholics. The British soldiers are supposed to be in Ireland keeping the peace between us and the Protestants. Which is fine, except the way it works out is the Brits are on the side of the Protestants. And it's us, the Catholics, who get the house-to-house searches at three o'clock in the morning, battering down our doors and pulling us from our beds and destroying everything they can put their filthy hands on while they pretend they're searching for a gun or a bomb."

Kevin Payne, as young as he was, said, "The English have no right in Ireland! Let them go back to their own country!"

"That's the good lad," said Brendan.

So they became rebels with a cause, and the grim, narrow streets in the Falls Road and Shankill areas, with their dirty, crumbling nineteenth-century houses, became their jungle and their battleground. They threw stones at British soldiers; they hurled gasoline bombs at the British Land Rovers and armored cars under the cover of night; they helped the young men, all unemployed, make nail bombs. They became young terrorists.

And as well as their British enemies, they also had the Irish Protestant militants and the Ulster police, who were mostly Protestants, after them. And if that wasn't enough, their own IRA, the provisional branch of the Irish Republican Army – or Provos as they were called – might take it into their heads to kneecap them for the mischief they got up to. Kneecapping meant you were crippled for life. Not that they had ever shot the knees or ankles of a child (ankles were a more popular target nowadays because of the greater pain and disability), but you could never tell – they seldom hesitated to impose their own brand of law and order among their own, even if it was the milder punishment of having a heavy concrete block dropped on your arm or leg until the limb snapped. Life was brutish and cruel.

His uncle drove on.

How many miles behind him to be retraced? Declan wondered. How would he ever find his way back? The farther they drove, the more impossible seemed his escape.

The road began to wind through a great forest; there were trees everywhere Declan looked, evergreens, he knew that much, but what kind they were he did not know and did not care. He felt tired and ... lost. The dark, brooding forest seemed to him a secret, unknown world, impenetrable and dark, and he was filled with the terrible numbness of despair.

They emerged from the forest into the brightness of sea and sky, but he closed his eyes and saw very little of it.

The road now twisted around coves and bays. Purple-gray rocks, jagged and dark, thrust themselves into the shining sea, but he merely glimpsed it. He sat with his eyes half-closed, exhausted. It was as though all the past weeks he had been fueled by a special kind of hatred that had pumped up his muscles and his sinews to a constant, explosive pitch, and only now had he let go, only now had his strength collapsed. He felt totally worn out. His head ached from the thioridazine; it felt like his brain was being crushed. His tongue was dry and swollen. He cared about nothing. He thought he would like to die.

▷ **16** *batter sth. down:* hit sth. repeatedly so that it falls down **18** *filthy:* dirty **22** *lad:* boy **23** *grim:* very serious and unpleasant **24** *Falls Road:* poor Catholic area in Belfast where only Catholics live · *Shankill area:* area where only working class Protestants live · *crumble:* decay, break apart **27** *armored* (NAmE) = (BE) *armoured:* covered by metal plates as a protection against attacks **34** *kneecap sb.:* shoot sb. in his/her kneecap (= Kniescheibe) **35** *mischief:* damage, harm **36** *ankle:* (Fuß-)Knöchel **38** *hesitate:* be slow or pause for a while because of uncertainty or unwillingness **38–39** *impose sth. among* (usu. *on*) *sb.*: force sb. to accept sth. **39** *brand:* type **40** *concrete:* Beton **43** *retrace sth.:* go back along sth. **50** *impenetrable:* impossible to get or see through **51** *numbness:* emptiness · *despair:* hopelessness **54** *cove:* kleine Bucht **55** *jagged:* not smooth, with a lot of tiny, often sharp edges · *thrust sth.:* push sth. forcefully **56** *glimpse sb./sth.:* get only a brief look of sb./sth. · *exhausted:* very tired **58** *sinew:* Sehne **59** *pitch:* degree, intensity

FIVE

Now that the rain has stopped, Matthew leaned over and opened Declan's window six inches. After awhile, the fresh air began to revive him, and by the time they were near their destination, Declan felt a little better.

Otter Harbour was more than a harbor, it was an entire village. There was Sawchuk's General Store, a service station, a couple of churches, a hotel, a post office, and a liquor store. There was a telephone booth outside the general store. A man waved at the truck as they drove by. Matthew waved back.

The house was not far past the Catholic church of Our Lady of Sorrows. Matthew turned into a gravel driveway, switched off the engine, and set the hand brake.

Although the effects of the drug had worn off, Declan felt exhausted. He was sleepily aware that the truck had finally stopped, and that there was a girl about his own age or a little younger standing at the back door with a young boy.

He climbed out of the truck and followed his uncle to the back of the house. By now, other people had come out to greet them. A tall, slim woman wiping her hands on her apron walked down the wooden steps and threw her arms around him and pressed him to her breast. She had a blue smudge on her jaw and smelled faintly of acrylic paint.

"Ah! It's wonderful you're here, Declan. I'm your Aunt Kate, but call me Kate."

Declan stood looking at her, his face expressionless. She had dark hair and blue eyes and a creased, smiling face, and wore a white shirt and dark skirt. She stood tall, with her shoulders back and her chin high, looking at him.

"Stand and let me take a look at you. Ah! It's the feeding up you need, you're as thin as a church mouse. Isn't it terrible starved the boy is, Matthew?"

His uncle stood, his long arms dangling at his sides. "Terrible starved, right enough."

"This is Ana," said Kate. The girl stood, waiting. All Declan noticed was that she wore a huge pair of sunglasses.

"Hi," she said, smiling.

Declan said nothing.

"And this is Thomas." Kate pushed the boy forward.

Thomas's way of welcoming Declan was to slap him several times lightly on the arm. He welcomed Declan like a puppy. "Hi, Declan," he said in the voice of a five-year-old, though his age must have been nearer nine or ten, for he was heavy and almost as tall as Declan. He had brown eyes and hair and wore jeans and a white T-shirt with something written on it.

Declan stared at Thomas.

"Have ye no bag?" said Kate.

Declan did not answer.

"Ah! Then come on in. There's dinner ready, and then you can rest. You must be destroyed for the want of sleep. It's the long journey, so it is."

Kate led the way back into the house. Declan heard her say to his uncle in a low voice, "Is it just tired he is? Or is there something wrong with the boy?"

"They had to tranquilize him," explained Matthew.

So that was why he felt so terrible! Declan felt a stir of anger.

"Is that the truth?" said Kate. "And the only clothes he has are the ones on his back?"

The girl, Ana, showed him where to wash and then took him up the high stairs to a room in the top of the house. "You can have this

▷ **2** *revive sb.:* bring sb. back to consciousness **3** *destination:* place a person intends to go **6** *service station* (NAmE) = (BE) *petrol station:* Tankstelle **11** *gravel:* small stones, usu. spread on paths or driveways **19** *apron:* piece of cloth worn for cooking **21** *smudge:* dirty mark often caused by rubbing · *faint:* slight, indistinct **30** *starve:* die from hunger **40** *puppy:* young dog

room," she said, "or you can take the one at the back, a floor down, same floor as me. Kate says it's whichever one you like."

The room was small, with a sloped attic ceiling, and had a window that looked out over the dark rocks and the ocean. The bed had an old-fashioned iron frame and was covered with a blue eiderdown quilt. He fell onto it. He still wore his tattered sneakers. He felt Ana touch him on the shoulder. He did not move. He felt her slip off his shoes and dimly saw her place them together by the chest of drawers. He closed his eyes.

He did not get up for dinner, but slept right through.

Sometime in the early hours of the morning, he was visited by his nightmare and awoke crying out when the bomb exploded.

And Kate Doyle was suddenly there, her arms around his shoulders, clasping him tight and crooning, "Ah! Hush now, everything is all right, it's all right, so it is."

But he pushed her away, wild, possessed by the devils of fear and frenzy. "Leave me alone!" And threw himself around and pulled the covers up over his head until she had gone away.

The wild ocean crashed on the jagged rocks, and from somewhere up on the hill came the lonely hoot of an owl.

SIX

Declan had slept the afternoon and the night away. Before six o'clock on Sunday morning, he swung his feet onto the floor and sat on the edge of his bed looking around the small room. Chest of drawers, painted white; small bedside table, varnished brown, with a gooseneck lamp; hardwood floor; blue rug at the end of the bed; wallpaper, yellow with some kind of a white latticework design; two seascape pictures on the wall; a narrow door on the wall opposite the window. He stood and walked over to the door and opened it: a closet, empty, with a shelf and clothes hangers. He closed the door.

Where was the bathroom? He went out onto the landing. The house was quiet. He padded down the stairs in his socks to the next landing. Which door? He tried one: a child's bedroom with Superman wallpaper. He found the bathroom on his second try. He went in and locked the door. The room was big, with bright lights and giant mirrors, not like a Belfast bathroom at all. He stared at the oddly shaped elliptical pink sink, the toilet bowl with its padded seat, and the unfamiliar bottles of shampoo and jars of God-knows-what. He ran the bath and stripped off his clothes. He had never seen himself so naked and illuminated. He climbed into the pink tub and soaked

▷ **3** *sloped:* schräg abfallend **5–6** *eiderdown quilt:* bedcover filled with soft feathers **6** *tattered:* torn (to pieces) **8** *chest of drawers:* Kommode **14** *clasp sb./sth.* [klæsp; BE klɑːsp]: hold sb./sth. tightly · *croon:* sing or hum in a soft, murmuring voice **17** *frenzy:* state of extreme excitement **24** *varnished:* lackiert **25** *rug:* small carpet **26** *latticework:* Gitter **29** *closet* (NAmE): cupboard **30** *landing:* Treppenabsatz **35** *odd:* strange **36** *sink:* Spülbecken **39** *illuminate sb./sth.:* brighten sb./sth. with light · *tub:* Wanne

for half an hour. He dried himself on the biggest towel he had ever seen, wrapped it around his lean body, grabbed his clothes, and hurried back upstairs to his room, where he put on the Jockey shorts and the loose white sweatshirt and thick work socks he found neatly folded on the top of his chest of drawers. His Aunt Kate must have left them for him while he was in the bathroom. He stepped into his old jeans.

He made his way downstairs and stood on the bottom step.

His aunt and uncle were in the kitchen, Kate working around the stove, Matthew sitting in a rattan easy chair reading a book. The room was big and bright, a combined kitchen-family room, with a round wooden table and six chairs. Beside his uncle's rattan chair was a small varnished table, its top crowded with a black telephone, a mug full of pens and pencils, and several magazines and books. Its lower shelf was filled with two thick phone books, one on top of the other. The walls were papered in the same kind of paper as in Declan's room – yellow and white.

Declan looked to the right. Opposite the kitchen there was a living room, also big – every room in this house was big. His aunt and uncle had not yet seen him. Declan walked into the living room. There was a wide stone fireplace flanked by two high bookshelves full of books and binders; an upright piano was set against the wall; there was a TV, a long brown sofa, old and worn, two matching chairs, two unmatched chairs – one a high-backed dark red velvet wing chair and the other a black-painted wooden rocker – and cushions of many shapes and colors. On the floor there was an Indian carpet. A long coffee table made of what looked to Declan like a giant tree knot that had been polished and varnished sat in front of the sofa. There were many paintings on the walls of trees and mountains, beach and sky, rocks and driftwood, ocean storms, all painted in a – what was it called, impressionistic? – style.

In Belfast, the first things you noticed in a Catholic home, thought Declan, were the pictures of the pope and Our Lady of Perpetual Succor and the Sacred Heart on the walls; they leaped out at you. But here it was different. His uncle and aunt had the usual pope in the kitchen and Sacred Heart in the living room, but perhaps because of the sheer size of the rooms, they were hardly noticeable. There were no holy pictures in his room now that he thought of it, only seascape paintings like the ones in the living room.

A door from the living room led out onto a front porch facing the ocean. The porch was wide and had a couple of old couches. Some of the couch springs had burst their way through the worn fabric.

Declan left the living room, walked past the stairs, and stood silently in the kitchen doorway. Kate pulled out a chair. "Ah, you're up. Sit yourself down, Declan, and I'll make you some Canadian pancakes. Ana and Thomas are not yet up. Is it tea you'd want, or coffee? We've become the great breakfast coffee drinkers, so we have …"

As she chattered on, she pulled gently at the neck and shoulders of Declan's sweatshirt the way his mother used to. She could not stand to see folds and creases in clothes that should be smooth, he remembered.

"… be sure to buy you some decent clothes tomorrow when the store is open, and shoes, the Lord knows you need shoes …" He leaned away from her touch with a shake of his shoulders, and she stood, empty hands suspended like hovering birds.

He looked at his uncle, relaxed, his big mournful face intent on his reading.

Kate turned away toward the stove. "And your hair needs cutting so it's out of your eyes. Matthew will cut it for you, he's a good barber."

He brushed the hair out of his eyes. "My hair is fine the way it is."

"We usually go to Mass at ten on Sundays," said Kate. "You'll meet Father O'Connor, and maybe a few of the children you'll be with on Monday."

"Monday?" said Declan.

"When you go to school," said Kate. "The bus picks up at the general store at eight-fifteen. Pender School is only ten minutes up the road. Or would you rather Tuesday? It'd give you the chance to get some clothes and look around a bit."

"Thanks," said Declan, "but I'll not be going to any school."

▷ **10** *easy chair:* Lehnstuhl, Sessel **13** *mug:* Becher **22** *binder* [ˈbaɪndə]: Aktendeckel **25** *rocker:* chair in which you can swing back and forth · *cushion:* Kissen **33–34** *Lady of Perpetual Succor* (NAmE) = (BE) *Succour:* Virgin Mary **40** *porch* (BE): veranda **49** *chatter* (v): talk quickly and continually about unimportant things **51** *crease:* wrinkle or line on clothes **56** *suspend:* hang · *hover* [ˈhɑːvər; BE ˈhɒvə]: remain in the air in one place **57** *mournful:* extremely sad **60** *barber:* hairdresser

Kate didn't pause in her mixing of the batter. "Not go, do I hear you say?" She shot a glance over at Matthew. "But what would you do with yourself around here? Ana is at the same school, and she says it's the great place. Ah! Wait and see, you'll like it just fine when you meet a few of the others."

"Good morning, good morning." An old lady came down the stairs dressed for the outdoors. She carried an umbrella and wore a blue Sunday coat with a little blue hat. She was thin and straight like a dry twig.

"Good mornin', Miss Ritter," said Kate. Matthew did not look up from his book.

Miss Ritter kept going straight for the door and waved the hand that was not carrying the umbrella. "Make yourselves at home," she said happily.

"She always goes to the seven o'clock Mass," Kate explained to Declan. She poured some of the batter into the pan.

Declan said, "You'd better know, both of you, I've no intention of staying here in Canada. I was forced to come." He shot an angry look at his uncle. "You had no right forcing me to come."

Matthew lowered his book. "It was my duty. I could do no less, Declan. You're my brother's son."

"You had no right to interfere!" insisted Declan.

"You've no one left in Ireland," said Matthew. "You will be better off here with your own, you'll see." He spoke quietly, almost in a whisper.

Declan spoke contemptuously. "My own are still in Ireland. Buried in Irish soil. Which is where I will be buried, too, after I've revenged their cruel murders."

Kate interrupted. "Sit at the table, Matthew, and have your breakfast." She placed two plates of pancakes on the table.

Matthew took his place opposite his nephew. Kate sat between them with her cup of coffee. "I'll maybe have a pancake myself when Ana and Thomas come down," she said.

"I was forced," said Declan, noticing Kate glance at the gold ring on his finger and the angry bruises on his wrists, "I wasn't asked."

Matthew poured syrup on his pancakes, then passed the bottle to Declan.

Declan poured too much syrup. "I'm needed in Ireland. At least I know my duty right enough. I'm not the kind who runs away from the battle like some I could mention."

"You haven't touched your coffee," Kate said to Declan. "I'll pour you a glass of orange juice." She got up and poured the juice while Declan and Matthew eyed each other across the table. "It's going to be the lovely day," said Kate. "After the church you can go for a walk, Declan. Ana and Thomas will show you around, won't you, Ana?" she said to the girl and the boy who had just come down the stairs.

"Sure," said Ana. She smiled at Declan.

Declan looked at her. She wasn't wearing her sunglasses now. About the same height as Declan and almost as thin, she had blonde hair, straight, chopped off flat at the jaw line. She wore a white T-shirt and a pair of blue denim cutoffs. Her skin was very tanned. She had pale green eyes and long blonde eyelashes. Her smile was warm and a little tilted, as though she were sharing a private joke that only she and he understood.

Thomas, he could see now, was one of those handicapped kids – what were they called? Mental retards or Mongoloids, something like that. His broad features looked to Declan like one large happy-face grin. Declan turned his attention back to his uncle.

"There's not much point looking round a place where I don't intend to stay," said Declan. He glared at Matthew. "Now that you know how I feel about being forced to come to this wild country, perhaps you will be kind enough to send me back. I'm well able to take care of myself."

Matthew put down his knife and fork on his plate and leaned his elbows on the table. "We want you to stay with us, Declan."

"Ah! We do!" said Kate. "Give it a chance. We need you to stay, Declan, so we do."

"I won't stay. If you won't send me back, then I'll make my own way back – somehow."

Matthew gave Kate a doleful look.

▷ **1** *batter:* Teig **2** *glance* [glæns; BE glɑːns] (n): quick look **9** *twig:* the thin part of a tree on which the leaves hang **22** *interfere:* concern oneself with sb. else's affairs without being asked to do so **26** *contemptuous:* looking down upon; despising **27** *soil* (fml): country, land **28** *revenge sth.:* return sth. (e.g. an injustice or injury) that one has suffered **50** *chop sth.:* cut sth. **51** *tanned:* brown from the sun **53** *tilt:* move into a sloping position **70** *doleful:* sad

* * *

The little chapel was crowded. Father O'Connor's sermon droned on and on without end.

In spite of all his sleep, Declan felt weak and tired. He wanted the service to be over so he could lie down somewhere, anywhere.

Sunbeams shone through the stained-glass windows, bathing the chapel in a rich, sleepy light. The pew was full. Ana sat on Declan's right, Thomas on his left. Ana had changed from T-shirt and cutoffs into a green dress. To Ana's right sat Matthew and Kate, Matthew stiff in his Sunday suit and Kate arty in a brightly colored, flowing caftan and a wide-brimmed straw hat festooned with artificial flowers.

Afterward, outside in the sunshine, Kate introduced Declan to the priest. Father O'Connor said how delighted he was to meet him and that when time allowed, he would love to sit and ask a few questions about Ireland. He seemed sincere. "And welcome to Canada," he said before they parted. Declan didn't answer the priest, so his aunt did it for him: "Thank you, Father," she said.

They walked home and changed into their workaday clothes.

Matthew settled into his comfortable chair in the kitchen with his book and a cup of coffee.

"Ana and Thomas will take you for a walk and show you around," said Kate.

"I prefer to be on my own," said Declan as he left the house.

He started making plans for his escape.

SEVEN

By the end of the day, he had a plan.

He would need money. He found two bills, a ten and a twenty, in the kitchen drawer where Kate and Matthew kept their letters and bills. He didn't like to take it, but he had no choice; they should have left him alone in Ireland and then he wouldn't need to steal their money. He had no idea how much thirty dollars was worth, but it would do; he would not need much, just bus fare and chocolate money, enough to keep him going for a couple of days until he got back home. He folded the bills and stuffed them into his uncle's coat, not the stained car coat, but a warm-looking padded ski jacket hanging beside it in the closet.

Next, he rooted through the glove compartment of his uncle's truck and found a map of British Columbia, which he stuffed into his pocket. He studied the map in bed that night. British Columbia was very big. He checked the scale of the map and the area of the westernmost Canadian province and did some rough calculations in his head. The whole country of Ireland would fit into British Columbia ten or eleven times! Imagine that! Ten Irelands! He shook his head in wonderment. He located Otter Harbour. The nearest town was called Sechelt. He located the Vancouver airport on Sea Island. He reckoned he should be able to make it by tomorrow night.

▷ **1** *drone:* talk in a monotonous voice **5** *sunbeam:* ray of sunlight **6** *pew* [pju:]: bench in a church **9** *arty* (infml derog): showing an exaggerated interest in art **10** *festoon:* decorate **14** *sincere:* honest **25** *bill* (NAmE): note, paper money **35** *root through sth.:* search hastily through sth. **44** *reckon* (infml): suppose, think

He left before dawn after a good night's sleep, before anyone was up. He tiptoed downstairs and helped himself to a couple of large hunks of his aunt's soda bread, which he stuffed into plastic bags. Then he slid the closet door open quietly, pushed the bread into the pockets of Matthew's jacket, the one with the thirty dollars in the pocket, and slipped the jacket on. A last-minute decision made him grab a green wool toque from the shelf and pull it on over his head. He listened for anyone moving upstairs. All was quiet. He crept out the door. He took nothing else except the map. It was a fine morning with no wind.

The jacket came down past his knees, but he had chosen it deliberately, knowing it would be warm. His vague plan was to get into the airport baggage room and somehow smuggle himself aboard the London flight in a trunk or large bag. But first he had to get to the airport. He did not know where he would be sleeping tonight and the jacket would be as good as a sleeping bag.

Besides, he'd need to wear something warm in the boat.

He had decided on the boat yesterday for several reasons. A boat was easy to start and easy to steal. The ones with outboard motors required no ignition key; all he had to do was pull the starter and he was on his way. Second, a boat would take him directly to the airport on Sea Island. Third, they would probably be looking for him on the road and at the ferry terminals; they would not be looking for a boat. He hoped. Unless of course, the boat owner discovered his boat missing and reported the theft to the police … .

He walked along the beach; the road would be deserted at this hour, but he did not want to take the chance that someone would see him.

Because of the forested hills to the east, dawn was slow to come to Otter Harbour, but by the time he reached the boat dock, the sky above the hills was stained pink and orange and he could smell the ocean and the forest. He felt his heart lift with excitement. He was going to make it; he knew it, he could feel it in his bones.

There was nobody at the boat dock. He climbed into the boat he had selected yesterday, a fiberglass runabout with a small canopy that would protect him from easy identification, just in case they were looking for him with binoculars; it would also keep off the rain and wind. He had checked the gasoline yesterday and the tank was almost full; he did not know how far it would take him, but if he followed the shoreline, he could always tie up at a dock and get more.

It was the first time he had ever been in a small boat. He did not feel as sure of himself today as he had felt yesterday when he had studied the motor.

He jerked the starter rope. The forty-horsepower outboard started after a few pulls. He untied the boat and pushed off. He slipped the motor into gear and twisted the throttle to low for a few minutes until he had a good direction, then once the dock was far behind, turned it to "full." The little engine roared, the prow of the boat rose up out of the water, and the dark green sea boiled behind him.

His heart lifted. He was on his way home.

The sky was lighter now and he could see the cliffs and beaches and the forest behind them quite clearly. He watched an eagle soaring over the trees and rocks with effortless grace. The sea was calm. God was with him. Maybe the eagle was God watching over him, guiding him home safely. Or that seal out there with its shiny nose and bristle whiskers poking up out of the water, swimming along near the boat. Was it his imagination, or did the seal give him a wink? Perhaps we are watched over by the dead, he thought. His ma, his sister Mairead, the da he did not remember, who died when he was only three, maybe they were all watching over him. He gave a sigh of satisfaction and sat back, enjoying the plunging motion of the boat, feeling the spray on his face, letting the powerful little motor do the work.

The sun came up and dissolved the mists from the mountains. He was too warm; he took off his uncle's jacket and the toque. He studied the map, trying to figure out from the shape of the coastline where he was. The big town he came to would be Sechelt. He kept heading south along the coast, looking for landmarks, checking his map periodically, lying back with the sun warm on his face, watching the

▷ **2** *tiptoe* (v): walk on the tips of one's toes **7** *toque:* Mütze **12** *deliberate* [dɪ'lɪbərət] (adj): done on purpose **20** *ignition key* [ɪg'nɪʃn]: key with which to start a car, boat, etc. **26** *deserted:* empty of people **35** *runabout:* small motorboat · *canopy:* small roof or shelter **46** *throttle:* Gashebel **48** *prow* [praʊ] (fml): front part of a boat **52** *soar* [sɔːr]: move in the air without using one's wings **55–56** *bristle whiskers* [brɪsl]: borstige Schnurrhaare **56** *poke (up) out of sth.:* be visible coming through sth. **57** *wink* (n): act of closing and then opening one eye quickly **63** *dissolve sth.:* make sth. disappear

other boats carefully. Whenever he came upon one fishing, he angled away from it so he could not be seen clearly.

After a few hours, he unscrewed the cap of the gas tank and checked the level by peering inside. About half a tank left. He figured he should be able to make it across Howe Sound before he had to stop to refuel. Which made him think about how the Holy Terrors used to siphon fuel from cars and trucks so they could make gasoline bombs to throw at the Brits. If only Brendan Fogarty could see him now!

He was now in open water, in the channel, he figured, between the peninsula and Bowen Island, feeling a little less certain of his seamanship. The wind had come up and the water was rougher. It was not cold enough to put on his coat, but he pulled the toque down over his forehead against a windburn. His arms and shoulders ached from holding the rudder, even though he tried to balance the load by switching from one side of the seat to the other.

He checked the gas again. Too low! Not enough to make it across the sound. He had not allowed for the strong headwind. The only solution was a stop at Bowen Island for gas. But what if there were no dock there, no boats, no fuel?

He stared at the island, misty in the distance, willing the motor to keep turning. Where was the eagle? Or the seal?

He was hungry. He ate one of the chunks of soda bread.

After awhile, he thought the motor sounded a bit different, as though it were thirsty. He was scared to take off the cap and look into the tank for fear he would find it dry. Keep going for another five minutes, he prayed, that's all, five minutes.

The boat heaved and rolled in the choppy sea. The motor coughed. He throttled back a bit. He was nearly there. He could see a narrow strip of beach where he could land the boat. He would have to be careful not to damage the motor. He examined its swivel mechanism and figured that he would have to pull the motor back and up out of the water when he could see the sandy bottom under the boat.

He was there! Up with the motor! The bottom of the boat scraped the sandy beach as he leaped out with the prow rope and dragged the boat up higher onto the beach, where the tide could not take it back again. It was a falling tide; the boat should be safe there a while.

He sat on the beach trying to decide what to do next. This could be a deserted island. His map was too small in scale to give any useful information. One thing was certain: The boat that had brought him here was no longer of any use to him. He would have to find another before he could continue his journey. Perhaps it was just as well. If he had put into shore at a dock on the peninsula, he might have been caught. And didn't bank robbers change cars to confuse the police? He stood up, hooked his thumb under the collar of the coat, slung it over his shoulder, and set off along the rocky shore, breathing a silent prayer to those watching over him not to desert him now, to let him soon find another boat.

▷ **7** *siphon* ['saɪfn]: absaugen **10** *peninsula* [pə'nɪnsələ; BE -sjələ]: Halbinsel **27** *choppy:* rough **28** *throttle back:* den Motor drosseln **30** *swivel mechanism:* Drehmechanismus **44** *sling sth. – slung – slung:* throw sth. carelessly

EIGHT

He walked for an hour along narrow trails, until he came to a headland and was forced to make his way up over the rocks.

When he had climbed up to the top, he could see for miles. There was no sign of a living soul, only a lone blue heron on the beach. Above the rocks and the trees and the glittering sea wheeled the screeching gulls. He looked up and saw an eagle gliding high in the sky above the cliffs and he took it as a sign.

He walked along the cliff intending to make his way over to the other side of the cape and then cut down to the beach again, but he thought he could hear something and stopped, listening. There was a noise, a rumble, that became louder over the cries of the gulls. It sounded like a truck. If it was a truck, then there must be a road or a trail.

He headed inland toward the noise, pushing his way through alder and salal brush. The truck noise died away, but he kept going and soon came to a gravel road running parallel with the coast. He turned south along the road, his sneakers crunching on the gravel.

The sun hung over his head at noon. He was thirsty. Why hadn't he thought to bring water instead of bread? Water was more important than food. Too late to remember that now. But there was bound to be water on the island, a stream or a creek; it had rained two days ago.

When he finally came upon a creek, channeled through a culvert under the road, he kneeled down and tasted the water. It was clear and sparkling and ice cold from the top of the mountain. He scooped up the water in his hands, slurping greedily. Then he lay back on a shady bed of ferns underneath a high canopy of hemlock trees and closed his eyes and rested.

There were no more cars or trucks. If a car did come along, he should hide; no good taking chances.

The air smelled sweet and pure. He could hear birds and the buzz of insects. It was all very calm and peaceful, the birds chattering and the tall trees rustling and the clear air shining. Eden must have been like this. He had forgotten what it was like in a forest or on a moor and only dimly remembered a trip he and his ma and Mairead had taken to the Donegal countryside when he was ten. Mairead would have been only seven. But he remembered the air and the silence.

He drank more water and then set off along the road once more. After awhile, the road dipped and curved downhill to a narrow junction, with another road running off to the right toward the coast. The new road showed signs of heavy usage. He would have to be careful he was not seen.

In ten minutes he was out of the forest and soon came to a collection of small cottages on the waterfront. There were a few cars and trucks and a dock with several boats. Two men stood in conversation on the dock. He heard the sound of a radio in one of the cottages playing rock music. This was the place, but he would have to wait for the men to leave.

He circled around the cottages, close to the trees, and worked his way toward the beach. He saw the men walking up the road away from the dock. They climbed into a truck and drove off.

He waited. It was quiet. He strolled casually onto the dock, hoping that if anyone saw him, they would not be suspicious. He had to be quick. He spotted an ignition key dangling from the dashboard of a small cabin boat. He was in luck! He threw his coat aboard and leaped down off the dock, ducking his head in under the cabin roof. His prayers were being answered. The seventy-five-horsepower

▷ **1** *trail:* path **4** *heron:* Reiher **6** *screech:* cry in a harsh voice **14** *alder* ['ɑːldər; BE 'ɔːl-]: Erle **15** *salal:* bush native to British Columbia · *brush:* land covered by small trees and bushes **21** *creek* (NAmE): small stream **22** *culvert:* Abwasserkanal **25** *slurp* (infml): eat or drink noisily · *greedy:* eager, with extreme hunger or thirst **26** *hemlock tree:* Schierlingstanne **32** *rustle:* rauschen **35** *Donegal* [ˌdɑːnɪ'gɑːl; BE -'gɔːl]: county in the west of Ireland **38** *dip:* go downwards **39** *junction* ['dʒʌŋkʃn]: point at which roads meet **51** *stroll* [streʊl]: walk in a slow, leisurely way · *casual* ['kæʒuəl] (adj): without much care or thought

outboard would get him there faster. He untied the boat and pushed off. When he had drifted out a short distance, he started the motor, slipped the transmission into gear, and nursed the boat along for a few hundred yards until he was well clear of the shore. He looked back. All seemed quiet. It had been too easy. His heart swelled. It was a moment of triumph. He opened the throttle and headed for Sea Island, singing loudly for joy over the crash of the spray and the roar of the powerful motor:

The minstrel boy to the war is gone,
In the ranks of death you'll find him;
His father's sword he has girded on,
And his wild harp slung behind him.

He kept away from other boats with their trailing fishing lines, circling around them as he had done before, but then almost out of nowhere came one of the huge blue-white ferries, large as an ocean liner, bearing down on him, bellowing madly like an angry sea monster.

The *Queen of Esquimalt* was heading for Horseshoe Bay.

His heart bottomed out. "BC Ferries" said the name on the smokestack. The thing was enormous. It howled constantly at him to get out of its path. The noise was deafening. In his panic to get away, he swung the wheel too hard and almost capsized the boat. Water slopped into the cabin. The motor protested, faltered as if about to stall, then recovered. He urged the boat out of the giant's path as the motor picked up power and speed. The ferry slid by only yards away, still screaming with rage. He turned the boat and throttled back, heading it into the waves that followed the ferry's passage. Again he almost capsized, as the boat heaved and swung in the violent afterwash.

He hung on to the wheel. When the waves had abated and his heart had stopped pounding, he opened the throttle again, this time watching the horizon more alertly.

He slipped his uncle's coat on. It was colder now. Clouds obscured the afternoon sun. He ate the remaining hunk of soda bread and consulted the map. That must be Point Grey in the distance, he decided. The motor sounded good. He would soon be there, an hour maybe.

He ran out of gas just off the point.

The boat wallowed helplessly only a few hundred yards from the shore. He was beginning to feel tired and dispirited; his arms and shoulders ached, and the bruises on his wrist felt sore. He rubbed his cold hands together, and rubbed at the gold ring on his middle finger.

He wasn't finished yet! He'd come this far. He would try to signal another boat and buy or beg enough gas to take him to Sea Island; it wasn't that far away.

He scanned the seascape for a boat close enough to see his signal, while the drift tide took him back around the point into the mouth of English Bay. A sleek sailboat was coming his way. He started to wave his green toque to attract attention but, startled by a sudden thumping noise behind him, turned his head and saw a high, menacing prow bearing down on him. It was the coast guard.

The forty-one-foot coast guard search-and-rescue vessel, *Osprey*, acting on a call from the *Queen of Esquimalt*, had been searching for a boy alone in a small boat. They had been searching for less than twenty minutes. It had not taken them long to find him.

▷ **3** *nurse sth.*: drive sth. with special care **9** *minstrel boy:* travelling composer, player and singer of songs and ballads in the Middle Ages **11** *gird sth.:* fasten with a belt around the body **12** *harp:* Harfe **16** *bear down on sb./sth.:* head quickly and threateningly towards sb./sth. · *bellow* (v): make a deep loud sound **20** *smokestack:* chimney · *howl* (v): make a loud, wailing cry **22** *capsize sth.:* cause sth. to be overturned **24** *stall* (v): stop suddenly **29** *afterwash:* waves caused by the movement of a ship **30** *abate:* become less **32** *alert:* attentive **33** *obscure sb./sth.:* hide sb./sth. from view **38** *wallow:* swim about helplessly **47** *sleek:* well-styled **49** *menacing:* threatening

NINE

The sign on his desk said *Arthur McKenzie. Coxswain.* He was a tough, grizzled man with a Scottish accent. He held a report in his hand as he glared at Declan across his desk. "You stole the boat from Bowen Island."

Declan said nothing.

"Where do you live?"

Declan stared at him.

"What's your name, son?" McKenzie's tone softened.

"Do you think I could have a drink of water?"

McKenzie called to one of the men in the next room to bring some water. Declan drank the water quickly; his mouth felt so dry.

McKenzie resumed his questioning: "What's your name?"

Declan held out the empty glass. "Could I have some more?"

McKenzie gave a sigh. "More water for Oliver Twist!" he yelled into the other room.

Declan drank the second glass of water and put the empty glass on McKenzie's desk.

"Well?"

Declan said, "Thanks."

"I was asking about your name."

Declan said nothing.

When Declan would answer none of the questions, McKenzie called the police. Five minutes later they were marching Declan out of the coast guard station and into their police car. There were two of them, uniformed. They pushed him into the backseat. There were no handles on the insides of the doors. By now it was getting dark. They whisked him to headquarters in downtown Vancouver, where he was handed over to a big man with a badly pockmarked face. He chewed gum. His dark jacket was badly crumpled. The sign on his desk said DETECTIVE SAM GORE.

Gore's office was small, with barely room for the desk and two chairs. Declan sat and hunched his shoulders. Gore sat back and stared at Declan with hard, unfriendly eyes, his jaw chewing rhythmically.

Declan sat, relaxed, eyeing the big detective.

Gore stared and chewed.

Declan allowed his gaze to wander about the office, but there was nothing to focus on, no notices, no pictures of Most Wanted Men, no pictures of any kind: The room was completely featureless. He brought his attention back to Gore.

Declan's indifference had made Gore angrier, his chewing jaw tighter, his stare now a hostile glare. He spoke, forcing the words out slowly between his teeth. "What's your name?"

Declan said nothing.

Gore stopped chewing. His eyes protruded. "You hear me, boy?" he growled in a strangled voice. "I asked your name!"

Declan said nothing. He watched the detective calmly.

Gore, barely controlling himself, gripped the edges of his desk with his big paws as if he were about to hurl it aside and attack Declan with his fists. "It's all the same to me, boy," he rasped, "but you could end up spending the rest of your life behind bars. So you better start talking, you hearing me?" He leaned forward over the desk. He was boiling. "You stcal a boat from Bowen; you get near killed by a ferryboat; you got no ID; and seems like you're deaf and dumb. Who are you, boy? What's your name? Where do you live? Why'd you steal a boat? You better spill it, before I get mean! And when I get mean, I'm like *mean*, man!"

▷ **1** *coxswain* ['kɑːksən; BE 'kɒks-]: (here) man in charge of a boat and its crew **14** *Oliver Twist:* reference to the novel by Charles Dickens, in which the character of Oliver Twist asks for more food when it is forbidden to do so **27** *whisk sb.:* move or take sb. quickly **28** *pockmarked:* showing scars from acne in one's youth **32** *hunch sth.:* bend sth. forward into a rounded shape **41** *indifference:* having no interest or feeling **42** *hostile* ['hɑːstl; BE 'hɒstaɪl]: extremely unfriendly, showing that sb. is considered an enemy **45** *protrude* [prə'truːd]: stick out **46** *strangled voice:* voice that sounds as if sb. is squeezing one's throat **50** *rasp:* say in an unpleasant voice **54** *ID:* identity card or something that shows who one is **56** *mean* (sl): nasty

"Up yours," said Declan calmly.

Gore howled with rage. "Why, you little snot!" He reached over the desk for Declan's neck.

The door opened. "Everything okay in here?" It was another detective. He stepped in quickly and held Gore by the arm. "Take it easy, Sam, he's only a kid. Look, why don't you go get a cup of coffee." He wrestled Gore out from behind the desk and pushed him out the door. "Leave the kid to me, okay?"

He came back, smiling, and put out his hand. "I'm Jake Ball." He had bad teeth. He also chewed gum.

Declan ignored the outstretched hand.

Ball kept smiling. "Let me help you, son. You're in a heap of trouble, but it's nothing that can't be put right. I want to help you, okay?" He had a very friendly face. He offered Declan a stick of gum.

Declan ignored the gum. "I'm not your son. And I've been through the bad guy-good guy routine before. With professionals. So save your breath."

Ball threw up his hands. "Okay. If that's the way you want it. If I let my partner in here again, he'll murder you, I know it. He's mean. But if that's what you want …"

"I'm trembling," sneered Declan.

Ball hurried out and closed the door behind him.

Declan sprang to the door. It wasn't locked. He opened it and walked through. He could see Ball talking to Gore in another room. He hurried down the stairs and out the door into the dark street. He ran.

His legs were cramped from all the sitting in the boat. Running was painful. He jumped on a bus, not knowing where he was going, but it did not matter; he wanted to put some distance between himself and the police station.

He handed the driver his ten-dollar bill.

The driver gave back the ten and said, "You have to have the change. Seventy cents."

"Huh?"

The driver jerked his head. "Forget it. Siddown."

He sat down beside an old man. "Does this bus go to the airport?"

"You want to get to the airport?" The old man seemed surprised that anyone would want to go there. "There's a bus goes every hour, on the hour …" He consulted his watch. "… You should just about make one." He pointed ahead. "Get off at the next stop, and walk over one block to the Vancouver Hotel. Bus goes every hour."

Declan thanked him.

Forty-five minutes later, he was at the airport terminal scanning the monitors for information on flights to Britain. There was one going to Prestwick tomorrow morning at eight. The name was familiar. Prestwick was in Scotland. Or England; he could not be sure. But it didn't matter which; either one would do, for Ireland was but a few hours away on the ferry. He drank from the water fountain. Then he bought two bars of chocolate and a bag of crisps – potato chips they called them here.

It was late and he was exhausted. It had been a long day. The waiting room was full of sleeping bodies. He would have to be careful: Matthew knew he would be making for the airport. Would hc be here searching for him? He drank from the water fountain again and then washed his hands and face in the washroom. After that he lay down on the hard terminal floor with the other overnighters. He ate his crisps and chocolate and wrapped himself up in his uncle's coat and slept.

* * *

He had not slept well. The floor was hard, and he woke often, pulling his coat over his head, worried that his uncle might be looking for him among the sleepers.

He got up, went to the washroom, had a long drink from the water fountain, then bought a packet of peanuts and a bottle of Coke. He ate the peanuts and swigged back the Coke.

By six o'clock the terminal was busy and alive again. He noticed a crowd of school kids wearing identical blue-and-orange sweatshirts with the name of their school, "Windermere." Many wore jackets over their shirts. He asked one of them where they were going. "Scotland," she said. She was about his own age and looked like Ana.

"What time is the flight?"

"Eight o'clock. Where are you going?"

"Scotland will do fine."

The girl laughed. "Are you serious? Do you have a ticket?"

▷ **21** *sneer* (v): höhnisch grinsen **35** *siddown* (sl): sit down **63** *swig sth. back* (infml): drink sth.

"No."

"Well, then?"

"Maybe I could smuggle myself onto the plane with your group."

"It's a charter flight," said the girl. She didn't look like Ana, really, now that she was up close. But there was something about her that was like Ana, maybe the combination of blondness and boldness, and the way she had of frowning so two vertical furrows appeared above her nose.

"Is that the teacher in charge?" said Declan, nodding toward a large, bearded man who was talking to some of the children.

The girl nodded. "Mr. McManus."

"Would you stay with me and talk to me as you move onto the plane? I'm sure I could sneak through."

She frowned. "You're really serious, aren't you?"

He said, "What's your name?"

"Lisa. What's yours?"

"Declan."

"We're a school band. Touring Scotland for two weeks."

"That's nice."

"If you like, I can get you one of our shirts. Then you'd look like the real thing."

"Thanks."

Lisa moved away through the crowd.

Declan looked around. No sign of his Uncle Matthew. It was hard to outguess his uncle. It looked like he had not reported him to the police as a runaway. And he didn't seem to be here, though you could never tell.

Lisa was back with the shirt. Declan slipped it on over his T-shirt. It was big on him.

"Thanks, Lisa. If I get caught I won't tell where I got this from, so don't worry."

Now he looked like one of them. All he had to do was keep away from McManus. He would keep his own jacket on for now, so it covered the Windermere shirt.

The Windermere group started moving into the departure gate at seven-thirty. Declan moved with them. He had no bag, so he walked quickly through the baggage checkpoint into the waiting area. Lisa sat beside him. The Windermeres were now mixed in with several hundred other passengers. Declan kept his jacket closed.

The call came for boarding. As he approached the boarding-pass checkpoint, Declan slipped off his jacket. He now looked like a Windermere. He stayed slightly behind Lisa. As Lisa handed in her boarding pass, she gave a cry and fell to her knees. The startled checker bent to help her. Declan slipped through without looking back. He clenched his jaw, expecting to hear the checker yell, "Hey, you!" but Lisa's little trick had worked. He was free to board the airplane.

He shrugged his jacket on in case the teacher should spot him. He was on the plane, the flight attendant at the doorway smiling at him, welcoming him aboard.

He moved in with his head down. Damn! His jacket caught on a seat arm in the narrow aisle and exposed his shirt. McManus was watching him from one of the aisle seats. Declan's heart skipped a beat. Had McManus seen the shirt? Declan would soon know. He took a seat at the rear of the plane, ready to move if someone else claimed it.

He stared out the window.

His heart was beating wildly. Another twenty minutes or so and he'd be on his way home.

He closed his eyes and said a prayer and thought about Brendan Fogarty's face and all the others' in the Holy Terrors when they saw him back home in the Falls Road. And Tim O'Malley next door, and Tim's ma and da, their eyes wide with shock and surprise. "Is it back you are?" Unbelieving, like seeing a ghost.

"Could I please see your ticket and your passport?"

It was a flight attendant, a dark man in a navy blue uniform.

His stomach sank.

What rotten luck! McManus had seen him. There was nothing he could do. He felt suddenly very weary, as though a great weight was pressing him down.

They took him to the immigration office.

It was the same man as before. Raghavji.

His eyes popped. "I know that boy!" he cried.

▷ **6** *boldness:* fearlessness **7** *frown* (v): move the eyebrows together to show disapproval · *furrow:* deep wrinkle **43** *startle:* surprise **45** *clench sth.:* press sth. firmly together **53** *skip sth.:* leave sth. out **55** *rear:* back part of sth. **68** *rotten luck* (infml): bad luck **69** *weary:* very tired **73** *pop* (fig): come out suddenly

TEN

Matthew looked tired. "I came as soon as I got the call."

It was three o'clock in the afternoon in Raghavji's office. Declan had been kept in a locked room for over six hours.

Matthew gave Declan one of his doleful looks. "I'll not be a jailer, Declan. If it's escape you want, then go. I'll not stand in your way."

"Then give me the money to pay my way back," Declan demanded.

Matthew shook his head. "I can't do that, because I want you to stay. You belong here now. This is your home."

"My home is in Ireland."

Matthew said, "We'd hoped you would take this country to your heart as Kate and I did."

"So if you wanted so much for me to stay," Declan sneered, "why is it you didn't come chasing after me to the airport?"

Matthew shook his head. "We telephoned the police to keep an eye out for you. We drove to the ferry terminal. Nobody remembered having seen you. We returned home and waited by the phone. That was a smart move – the boat." He allowed himself a small smile. "You're the bold man – the spit of Liam, your father."

"Too bold and too much of a handful for you! You don't want me here. Let me go home."

"I'll make a deal with you. Stay with us until the end of March, and if you still want to go, then I'll not stop you. I'll pay your way back."

"You'll pay my way back?" Declan couldn't think. He felt weary.

"Come back with me now," said Matthew. "We can discuss it with Kate tomorrow."

"What if I don't come back with you?"

Matthew shrugged. "Then I'll leave you here."

Declan felt tired and defeated. There seemed to be no way out of the trap he was in. Perhaps the only way was to accept his uncle's offer of a deal. They drove back to Otter Harbour. He slept uncomfortably in the old truck most of the way.

Kate was waiting for them with hot chocolate to drink. "Will you eat a bite of the blueberry pie?" she asked Declan. She was happy to see him back.

Declan handed her the twenty-dollar bill and change. "I took this."

She dropped the money in the drawer. "We were destroyed worrying about you, Declan, love."

* * *

The next morning at breakfast, Declan said to Matthew, "Let's talk about this deal of yours." Ana and Thomas were not yet up. Kate sat down with her coffee.

"Stay with us to the end of March," said Matthew. "Then if you still feel you want to go back to Ireland, I'll pay your way."

"March is over six months away!" said Declan. "That's too long." He thought for a moment. "Make it the end of next month, October."

Matthew said, "Be reasonable, Declan. We want you to stay for as long as possible so you'll get to like it here. Tell you what, stay to the end of February."

"End of November," said Declan. "I'll not stay longer."

Matthew shook his head. "To give Otter Harbour a proper chance needs at least six months. But I'll accept end of January."

"No! November," said Declan. "That's my final word."

"January," said Matthew. "That's *my* final word."

They eyed one another, Declan defiant, Matthew stubborn, both equally determined.

"How do I know I can trust you?" said Declan. "How do I know you'll keep your word?"

▷ **4** *jailer:* prison guard **13** *chase after sb.:* run after sb. in order to catch them **18** *the spit of sb.* (dialect) = *the spitting image of sb.:* close copy of sb. **28** *defeat sb.:* win a victory over sb. **46** *reasonable:* vernünftig **54** *defiant:* [dɪ'faɪənt]: disobedient · *stubborn* ['stʌbən] (adj): determined not to give in

Kate was horrified. "Declan! I'll not allow you to speak to your uncle like that! In his own house! God strike me dead if I'm telling a lie, but Matthew never broke a promise in his life."

There came a clatter on the stairs.

"November," said Declan. "I'll not be ..."

"Good morning," said Miss Ritter on her way out the door. "It's another lovely day."

"It is," said Kate.

"Help yourselves to the cookies," Miss Ritter sang as the door closed behind her.

Declan stared at the closed door angrily, then glared at his aunt. "Who *is* that old woman?"

"Miss Ritter," said Kate. "She has the room next to Ana's. She's always the cheerful one, isn't she, Matthew?"

But Matthew, his mind still on the argument, wasn't listening. "You're the stubborn man," he said to Declan quietly. "But I'm just as stubborn as ye! I said January and January it will be." He pushed away his empty plate and started to rise from the table.

"Wait," said Kate. "I have the solution. Make it after Christmas and make it a part of the deal that Declan go to the school."

"Huh?" said Matthew.

"It's a deal," said Declan before his uncle could object.

There came a patter of bare feet on the stairs as Ana and Thomas tumbled down into the kitchen together, laughing.

"Welcome back, Declan," said Ana, smiling.

"Back, Declan," said Thomas, a huge grin on his face.

"You've been sitting on the stairs listening," Kate accused them.

They laughed.

Declan looked at Ana. Her pale green eyes looked back at him with a sparkle that told him she had heard every word of the deal he had made with his aunt and uncle.

After breakfast Ana declared a private holiday, refusing to go to school.

"What ails you, girl?" said Kate. "Have you lost your senses?"

"Declan's back," she said. "We decided to celebrate, didn't we, Thomas?" Thomas, still grinning, nodded vigorously. Ana turned to Declan. "Come for a walk with us along the beach. Then after that we'll show you where the otters live, and there's a deep pool with an octopus."

Declan shrugged.

They started out. Ana wore her big sunglasses.

Thomas danced excitedly around Declan, making whooping noises.

"You've made Thomas happy, coming back," said Ana, "you really have."

"Hmmph!" said Declan.

"Hmmph yourself," said Ana.

▷ **17** *ye:* you **30** *sparkle:* flash of light **34** *What ails you?* (old-fashioned IrE): What troubles you? **36** *vigorous:* energetic **42** *whoop* [hwu:p; BE wu:p]: utter a loud cry, expressing joy or excitement

ELEVEN

They scrambled down the rocky cliff in front of the house and walked along the beach. Thomas tagged along behind, happy to be a follower.

"Who is Miss Whatsername, the old lady who lives upstairs?" said Declan.

"Miss Ritter? She came about the same time I started in second grade – that's about five years ago – when her house burnt down. She forgets things." Ana laughed. "Poor Miss Ritter. Most of the time she thinks she's still in her old house, she really does. Believes we've all come to visit her. She's kind of hilarious, don't you think? Matthew put in a little kitchen for her with a little hot plate surrounded by that safety stuff ..."

"Asbestos."

"Right. So she's pretty independent. Only thing we have to worry about is her burning the house down. I've got the job of chief sniffer – because my room is next door. If I smell anything burning, I'm supposed to holler."

Ana picked up a thin piece of driftwood and wrote her name in the sand in letters a foot high. Then she handed it to Declan, to write his name beside hers, but he threw it up in the air at a passing gull. Ana gave him a bruised look.

"Sorry," said Declan, "but this is not my country for me to be putting my name on."

Thomas ran and fetched the driftwood. He tried to write his name in the sand. Ana helped him. They stood back and admired their handiwork. Thomas laughed happily.

"Your name is spelled with only one *n?*" Declan said to Ana. He could see he'd hurt her and was sorry.

"That's right. I need only one."

They walked in silence.

"How old are you, Ana?"

"Twelve. I know how old you are – thirteen. And I also know you lost your mother and your sister."

They stopped at the edge of the ocean and stood for a while looking at the breakers rolling in. Declan had his hands in the pockets of his jeans. Ana picked up a stone and threw it into the sea. Thomas copied her and started collecting more stones, yelling happily as he threw them into the surf.

"It was a bomb explosion, wasn't it?"

"I don't want to talk about it." He hadn't talked to anyone about the bomb, not even the O'Malleys.

"It might do you good to talk. That's what Kate always says and she's right. It was in a shop wasn't it, when your mother was shopping?"

Declan was silent for awhile, seeing for the umpteenth time the images from his nightmares. "No," he said.

"Where, then?"

He considered. Ana was looking at him. He met her eyes. "It was a restaurant, one of those posh places where ladies go for tea and buttered scones. They'd never been there before; it was a treat."

They continued along the beach. Hungry gulls screeched and wheeled overhead, and high on the cliffs black cormorants dried their wings. Thomas was still throwing stones into the sea. Ana yelled back at him, "Come on, Thomas." She turned again to Declan. "Do you want to tell what happened? You don't have to, you really don't, but ..."

As they walked, he told her the whole story.

His ma and Mairead had been sitting at a window table in Ford's Tea Room. It was Mairead's birthday, and she was drinking tea with

▷ **2** *tag along:* follow closely **9** *hilarious:* very funny **16** *holler* (NAmE infml): yell, shout **17** *driftwood:* wood washed ashore by the sea **24** *admire sb./sth.:* regard sb./sth. with pleasure or respect **34** *breaker:* waves that turn to foam when they reach the shore **44** *umpteen* (infml): too many to count **48** *posh* (infml): very elegant and expensive **49** *scone* [skɒn, skəʊn]: sweet small plain bun or roll · *treat:* thing that gives great pleasure and is done rarely

her ma and eating a chocolate eclair, taking care not to drop any chocolate or spill any tea on her new white wool sweater. She was a happy, normal little kid of ten, taking a day off school and shopping with her ma on her birthday.

"How do you know they were sitting by the window? And how do you know Mairead was eating a chocolate éclair?"

"I don't. I wasn't there; I was at school. But that's usually the way I see it." He frowned. "Her white sweater was a birthday gift. Sometimes when I go over it in my head, the details change a bit: Sometimes Mairead is eating ice cream with a spoon, and my ma is talking to her and waving a piece of strawberry cheesecake on the end of a fork."

By this time they had reached the dock where the boats were tied up. Declan felt the sun warm on his face. They sat together on the bottom of an upside-down herring skiff.

"The bomb exploded at ten o'clock in the morning," continued Declan.

Six people, including Mairead and their ma, Mary Doyle, were killed instantly, two more died on the way to the hospital, and twenty-two people were injured, eight of them seriously.

"Who did it?" said Ana.

"The dirty Prods!"

"The Protestants?"

"That's right."

It was the police who came to the school with the news. He was called out of his last-period history class to go to the headmaster's study. As he walked along the corridor and down the stars, he wondered what he had done to arouse the interest of the Head. This of course was before he joined the Holy Terrors, when his worst sin up to then had been thinking impure thoughts about Bridget Fahey, the most beautiful girl in the school, though he didn't tell this part to Ana.

"You joined a gang?"

"That's right."

"Why?"

"Because the Holy Terrors are sworn to fighting the British. And fighting the Protestant militants. And fighting the police, too. We have three enemies: the Brits, the Prods, and the police. We're freedom fighters."

When he saw the policeman standing beside the headmaster's desk and the headmaster himself sitting with his head bowed, the first thing Declan thought was that he was about to be accused of something he hadn't done.

The policeman told him quietly about the bomb, and the headmaster said he was sorry and to let him know if there was anything he could do to help. Was there anyone else at home? No, his da was dead; there was only the three of them, Mary Doyle, Mairead, and himself. He would be all right, he told the headmaster; there was Mrs. O'Malley next door if he needed anything. They wanted to send someone with him, at least to Mrs. O'Malley's. He said no.

He had gone home to an empty house.

When he had finished talking, Ana sat a little closer to him on the skiff. "When did your father die?"

"About ten years ago. I was only three. They killed him, too. With a gun."

Ana flinched. "Declan, you'd be crazy to go back there. All that killing. You really would. You gotta stay here; you can't go back!"

He shook his head. "You don't understand. The Irish people have been fighting for their freedom for hundreds of years. Just like the blacks in America. I'm needed.

"I've no choice. Besides, I want to get them – I've got to get them – for my sister and my ma. I've got to go back."

"Oh, I understand all right," said Ana, her voice heavy with irony. "I understand that you want to go back to all that killing. Look, I feel sorry about your family, Declan, but you've still got your own life to live. Killing people isn't the answer!"

"It's my life," he said angrily.

"If you call hating and killing a life."

"I should have known you wouldn't understand."

Ana bristled. "Maybe I'm younger than you, Declan, but in lots of ways I'm much older. I understand a lot more than you think I do."

"You understand nothing!" He jumped up and started back along the beach toward the house.

Thomas ran. "Wait up, Declan!" he called to Declan's stiff back.

"Stay with your know-it-all sister!" yelled Declan.

▷ **2** *spill sth.:* etwas verschütten **15** *skiff:* small rowing boat **56** *flinch:* move back suddenly due to shock or pain **70** *bristle* ['brɪsl] (v): show anger

* * *

When Declan got back, he found his uncle in the old clapboard garage, bent over his workbench, tinkering with a television set.

Declan looked around. The garage was full of old toasters, TV sets, electrical appliances of all kinds. Many had been cannibalized for their spare parts. There were bicycles and parts of bicycles, and junk of every description; in the corner where Matthew had his workbench there was an electric heater.

Matthew looked up from the TV set.

"So this is what you do? Repair TVs?" Declan leaned on the end of the workbench.

Matthew nodded and waved a hand around the cluttered garage. "I fix things."

"People, too? Do you fix people, too? You fixed me right enough, dragging me over the top of the world and setting me down in your British Prison Columbia. You're the great pair of fixers, you and my aunt!"

"We made a bargain. Your sentence expires in just over three months. When the time comes, you are free to go. I will pay your way as I promised."

"Three months! You sure sucked me in with all that talk of six months. I see now the pair of you had it all planned. 'Make it after Christmas,' " Declan mimicked his aunt.

"A bargain is a bargain."

"I'm beginning to regret it. How can I trust you? Didn't you have me kidnapped? And any man who would leave poor Ireland to solve her own troubles is not a man to be trusted."

"In Ireland they kill one another. Killing solves nothing, Declan. Blood begets more blood."

"Swear an oath on the death of my da!"

Matthew sighed and raised his big hand. "I swear on the death of my brother Liam, your da."

"That you'll pay my way back home after Christmas."

"Home after Christmas." Matthew turned back to the TV set.

TWELVE

Pender was a small school. Mr. Taylor, the principal, told Declan they would start him in ninth grade and arrange for his records to be sent from Ireland.

"Don't bother," said Declan. "I won't be here long."

"Where will you be?" Mr. Taylor was a stern man with piercing blue eyes and a way of tilting his head slightly to one side when he asked a question.

"Back home."

"Ireland is still your home? But I understood you have no relatives living there."

"No relatives, but Ireland is my country and the Irish are my people."

Mr. Taylor studied the form on his desk. "You are now living with your aunt and uncle in Otter Harbour?"

"Until Christmas."

Mr. Taylor smiled. "Give us a try. I think you will like it here, Declan."

Declan scowled. "Will there be anything else?"

Mr. Taylor placed the form in his desk tray. "That's everything. Let me know if there's any way I can help you settle in."

▷ **1** *clapboard* (NAmE): Verschalungsbrett **2** *tinker with sth.:* try to repair sth. in an inexpert way **4** *appliance:* instrument for a special purpose **5** *junk* (infml): things considered to be of little value **17** *bargain:* agreement, deal · *expire:* end **20** *suck sb. in* (infml): fool sb. **28** *beget sth.* (fml): cause sth. **29** *oath:* formal promise or declaration that sth. is true **35** *record:* permanent written account of facts or events **38** *stern:* serious **51** *scowl:* look at sb. with an angry expression

"Thanks, but I've no intention of settling in to anything British." He got up and grasped the knob of the door. "Especially your British Conundrum Columbia!" He did not wait for a reply, but closed the door behind him and wandered down to the school cafeteria, where he saw Ana chattering with two girls.

She saw him and came over. "I'm sorry I lost my temper yesterday, Declan." She smiled. "Kate is right; she's always telling me I shouldn't poke my nose into other people's business."

Declan shrugged his shoulders.

Ana introduced him to her friends. Declan nodded at them both briefly and left to buy a sandwich. When he got back, the trio had grown into a group, all girls, gathered around Ana's end of the table. As he hovered at the edge he heard, "… really good-looking, but …"

"But what, Leah?" Ana's voice.

"Well, he's awfully serious."

"So what's so bad about serious?" Ana again. "It's better than some of these clowns who never stop grinning and smirking."

"And he acts kinda … stuck-up, don't you think?"

"No, I don't think, Leah. He's just … shy. It will take a while for him to get used to things here."

They saw him and started talking about one of the teachers.

A few of the boys made fun of his accent, but Declan ignored them, and soon, after a week or so, they let him alone. All except a hulk of a boy named Lyle Dybinski, who was in eleventh grade. Dybinski had small, mean-looking eyes and thick rubbery lips. He was a bully, using his weight and height and his tough, aggressive appearance to get his way with everyone. He glared threateningly at students and teachers alike. He was so big and mouthy that even some of the teachers tried to stay out of his way.

"What language is that, eh?" he would ask his two followers, Al Barber and Leo Quiller, whenever they overheard Declan talking to someone. "Irish, I guess," one of them would say. "Sounds to me like pig grunts," Dybinski would say with a sneer. Or he would ask, "What did the Irish kid say, guys?" and Al or Leo would dutifully come up with some appropriate insult like, "Sounded to me like he was puking, eh?" They would all laugh. Barber and Quiller were small in comparison to their leader, Dybinski, and followed him everywhere like a pair of tiny, parasitic fishes under the belly of a killer shark.

Declan controlled his anger and tried to hide his growing distress and frustration.

At other times Dybinski kept his friends amused by yelling rude remarks like, "Well, if it isn't the IRA kid. Look out for bombs in your lockers, eh?"

On Thursday of the second week, Declan's lab partner in science, a dark, silent boy with the strange name of Joe Iron Eagle, glowered at him and said, "You're no help. I might as well do the work alone for all the good you are."

"Huh?" said Declan. Iron Eagle had black hair and glittering eyes and a nose like an eagle's, hooked and mean-looking. Maybe that was why *eagle* was in his name. He looked tough.

"You watch me do all the work," said Iron Eagle quietly, "then you let me write it up. Sometimes you don't even watch; you read your book."

Declan shrugged. "So complain to the teacher, why don't you?"

Joe looked at him levelly for a few seconds. Then he turned back to his work.

The next day, Iron Eagle said, "Dybinski is getting to you, right?"

Declan said nothing. He couldn't tell if his lab partner was about to ridicule him; besides, he had no intention of discussing his problems with this mean-looking character, who had said practically zero to Declan in the week or so they had been together.

Iron Eagle asked no more questions. He was silent.

The third week, Declan said to Iron Eagle, "Give me that. I'll write it up for you."

"Don't do me any favors."

"I won't." Declan took the pen and notebook and started writing.

"Ignore him," said Iron Eagle.

"Hmmnn?"

"Dybinski. Don't let him see he's getting to you. He'll soon quit."

▷ **3** *conundrum:* Rätsel **6** *lose one's temper:* get angry **12** *gather:* come together **17** *smirk:* sneer **18** *kinda* (sl infml): kind of · *stuck-up* (infml): arrogant **23** *hulk:* huge person **25** *bully:* person who uses his or her strength or power to frighten or hurt weaker people **34** *dutiful* (fml): obedient **35** *appropriate:* suitable; proper **36** *puke* (sl): vomit **44** *lab* (infml): laboratory **45** *glower at sb./sth.* ['glaʊər]: look at sb./sth. in an angry way **50** *tough:* strong-willed **55** *level* (adj): steady **59** *ridicule sb.:* make fun of sb./sth. **69** *quit* (infml): stop

The next day, Dybinski and his two friends followed Declan to the cafeteria, talking in loud voices so Declan and everyone else could hear. "It's the Irish kid," said Dybinski in mock surprise. "I thought by now the little runt would've quit school, his language problem being what it is."

"Not necessarily," said his friend Quiller. "We've got a very good ESL class for foreigners."

Barber joined in with, "That's right. Irish will be speaking English before the summer, wait and see!"

They laughed loudly and jostled one another.

In science that afternoon, Joe said, "Stay cool. They'll soon give up if you ignore them."

But they didn't stop.

By the end of the fourth week, Declan decided he'd had enough of Dybinski's so-called humor, so he waited until he saw him walking along the empty hallway on his way to the washroom during a class period and slipped out of his own class to follow him. He caught up to him at the water fountain.

Declan said, "No more of your crude jokes, Dybinski, okay? You've had your fun, but now it's time to stop."

Dybinski grinned and wiped his lips with the back of his hand. "Crude jokes? Me? Who d'ya think you're talking to, Irish?"

"My name is not Irish, it's Declan. Lay off me, that's all."

"And if I don't?" Dybinski puffed out his chest and drew himself up so that he was a full head and shoulders taller than Declan.

Declan looked up at him. "I'm asking you politely, with nobody else around, to leave me alone."

Dybinski's thick lips curled in a sneer. "You cowardly little turd!"

Declan clenched his fists so tight they almost squeaked. "Don't push me, I'm warning you."

"Cheeky Irish trash! Nobody threatens Lyle Dybinski, nobody, eh! I could tear you in two and rip your balls off."

Declan said nothing more, but turned on his heel and returned to class.

At the end of the day, Ana was waiting for him outside the school. So was Dybinski, with Barber and Quiller by his side.

"It's the IRA kid!" yelled Dybinski so everyone could hear. "Look out for a car bomb! Check under your hood before you drive off, eh!"

Declan walked over to him and jerked his head. "Come on. Let's get this over with." He turned toward the football field.

Dybinski and his two friends fell in behind him and followed, still jeering. Behind them a small crowd was gathering.

Then everything happened at once.

Declan made a sudden turn and lunged at Dybinski, taking the big bully completely by surprise.

Barber and Quiller fell back in astonishment.

Declan grabbed Dybinski's chest, his hands bunched in the bigger boy's sweater, and lunged forward with lowered head like a charging ram, pulling Dybinski's face down onto the top of his own head, butting him quickly and viciously. It was all over in under three seconds.

Dybinski let out a scream of pain as his nose broke and the blood gushed down his mouth and chin; at the same time he fell backward to the ground as Declan released the grip on his chest.

Declan stepped back, and when he saw that Dybinski was not about to get up, scowled at his two followers. "That was a Belfast kiss. Anyone else like one?"

Nobody else did. Barber and Quiller looked at each other and shrugged as though Dybinski was no concern of theirs.

"That was dirty fighting!" screamed Dybinski from the ground, holding his head back, trying to stop the flow of blood.

"All fighting is dirty!" yelled Declan furiously as he walked away. "Didn't you know that?"

He looked around for Ana, but she must have gone home.

She did not speak to him until the next day.

▷ **3** *mock* (adj): not real **4** *runt* (derog): insignificant or worthless person **7** *ESL* (abbr): English as a Second Language **10** *jostle sb.:* push roughly against sb. **24** *chest:* upper front part of the body from neck to stomach **28** *cowardly* (adj): lacking courage · *turd* (vulg): (here) unpleasant person **31** *cheeky:* lacking respect · *trash* (NAmE infml derog): person one does not respect **42** *jeer at sb.:* laugh at sb. **44** *lunge:* move forward quickly and suddenly **46** *astonishment:* great surprise **47** *bunch sth.:* fasten sth. together **48** *charge:* attack **49** *ram:* Schafbock **53** *gush:* flow in great quantities

THIRTEEN

The next day, Declan was called to the principal's office and asked to account for his violent behavior. "I will not tolerate fighting at this school," said Mr. Taylor. "There is no excuse for the injury you've done Dybinski. You broke the boy's nose and he had to go to the hospital in Sechelt."

"He had it coming."

"Fighting is no way to solve a problem."

Declan said nothing.

"Is it, now?" Mr. Taylor tilted his head, waiting for an answer.

"Yes," said Declan angrily. "It is. Sometimes that's all there is left."

Mr. Taylor gave him five detentions, to be served picking up litter around the school. "If there's any further fighting, Declan, I will have to suspend you."

"So suspend me!" Declan sneered, slamming the door as he left.

He was suspended for five days.

"I've had a call from the school," Kate said to Declan that evening after dinner. They were all sitting in the living room. Her voice was flat and hard. "It was the principal, Mr. Taylor. You've been suspended for a week. You've sent a boy to the hospital. And they say you're doing no classwork." She turned her eyes to the ceiling. "I said a prayer to the Holy Virgin that the boy will be all right."

"It was only a broken nose," said Ana.

Kate sucked in her breath. "*Only* a broken nose!"

"Now, Juno," said Matthew, "there's no need ..."

"You needn't Juno me, Matthew Doyle," said Kate angrily, jumping up from the wing chair and throwing a sweater around her shoulders. She sat down again, her face flushed with anger.

Declan was surprised at Ana's speaking up for him; she had been cool to him ever since the fight.

"You were fighting?" said Matthew to Declan.

Ana spoke up again. "Everyone thinks the boy deserved it. He really did. He's a big bully, three years older than Declan and a ton heavier. Everyone says he's been giving Declan a bad time ever since he started school." Ana flashed Declan a tilted, apologetic smile. "So it wasn't Declan's fault."

Kate said quickly, "Bully or not, there was no need to break the boy's nose!"

"Nobody feels sorry for him," said Ana. "He had ..."

Kate said, "Please go to your room, Ana, or go outside. Take Thomas with you. Matthew and I would like to speak to Declan alone for a minute."

Ana pulled a face, but got up and left.

When Ana and Thomas had gone outside, Kate turned to Declan and said sharply, "You made a deal that you'd go to school! You've been there barely five minutes, and already you're to miss a week! What kind of a bargain is that?" She sat upright in her chair, arms folded, jaws clenched. To Declan, she looked more formidable than the school principal.

"I can't help it if ..."

"Don't give me that 'I can't help it' excuse! You were rude and disrespectful to Mr. Taylor. Isn't that right?"

Declan was silent for a moment. He looked at Matthew, but saw no help there. He said to Kate, "He made me lose my temper."

"Mr. Taylor made you lose nothing," said Kate impatiently. "The fault was your own, Declan!"

▷ **2** *account for sth.:* explain the cause of sth. **6** *have it coming* (sl): deserve to suffer the unpleasant consequences of one's actions **11** *detention:* punishment of being kept in after school · *litter:* rubbish **13** *suspend sb.:* (here) not allow sb. to attend school **24** *Juno:* reference to the play *Juno and the Paycock* by Sean O'Casey, in which Juno is characterized as a suffering mother and wife **27** *flush:* turn red due to anger or embarrassment **47** *formidable:* impressive

The room was full of shadows. But Declan could see the anger and concern in Kate's clear blue eyes, and it was as if he were looking into his mother's eyes, and he couldn't understand why he felt like crying.

Kate waited until her anger subsided, then she spoke slowly and firmly. "You will go back to the school tomorrow, Declan, and you will go straight to Mr. Taylor's office, and you will apologize to that man for your rudeness. Then you will ask him if you may be allowed to accept the punishment he first gave you, before you were so disrespectful."

"It was to pick up trash around the outside of the school!" Declan was indignant. "I'm no trash collector! They would all see me and laugh!" He appealed to his uncle with open hands and staring eyes.

Matthew said nothing.

"You made a bargain," said Kate. "If you must pick up trash so you can keep that bargain, then pick up trash you must."

Declan appealed silently again to his uncle.

"Kate is right," said Matthew.

Declan stood. "All right," he said to Kate. "I'll do it. But what if Mr. Taylor won't change his mind? I'll have to stay out for a week."

Kate's face softened. "Mr. Taylor is a fair-minded man. If you control your temper, Declan, and you are open and honest with him, then I see no reason why he'd let you miss school."

Thomas came clumping in from the outdoors and threw himself into a chair.

Matthew insisted on examining Declan's head to make sure there was no serious injury from the fight. "Anyone would think you were a rutting stag," he said.

Declan brushed the hair out of his eyes.

Matthew pressed. "Does that hurt?"

"No."

Matthew looked at him, his sad face longer and sadder than usual, if that were possible. "The Bible says if someone strikes us we should turn the other cheek!" he said quietly. Kate, talking now with Thomas, was not listening. Matthew pressed again. "Here?"

"Ouch! No. The Bible also says an eye for an eye and a tooth for a tooth," whispered Declan. "If you let people walk all over you, then you're a coward and a slave. It's easy to see why you ran away from the Irish struggle for freedom."

Matthew finished his examination. “Your head seems to be in one piece.”

Thomas wanted Matthew to examine his head also. He sat on Matthew’s lap. When Matthew declared him to be in one piece, he slid down and threw his arm affectionately around Declan’s shoulders and smiled with happiness, pulling him by the sleeve, wanting Declan to go with him.

“He wants to show you his things,” said Kate.

Declan followed Thomas upstairs to his room. It was the one with the Superman wallpaper. Thomas pulled an old suitcase from under his bed. He opened the case and started to take things out and hand them to Declan for inspection and approval. There was a green Sesame Street doll that took up most of the room in the box, several Superman and Batman comics, a handful of colored marbles, and a plastic soldier in khaki uniform and helmet thrusting forward with his rifle and bayonet. The helmet had a snap and could be taken off.

“An English soldier,” said Declan, “doing his dirty work.

Thomas caught the tone of disapproval in Declan’s voice and looked disappointed.

“But it’s good to have,” said Declan, smiling. “You can always piss in his helmet.”

“Huh-uh?”

“In his hat.” Declan made a gesture.

Thomas laughed. “Pissss!” Trying out the new word. Then he took a long white goose feather out of his suitcase. He stroked Declan’s cheek gently with the feather. Declan took the feather and tickled Thomas under the chin. Thomas giggled.

When Thomas had shown Declan all his things, he closed the suitcase and pushed it back under his bed. Then Declan showed Thomas the gold ring on his finger and told him it had been his ma’s. “It’s the only thing I have that I can show you, Thomas,” he told him.

* * *

“I was proud of you today, Declan.” Tilted smile.

▷ **4** *subside:* become less **11** *indignant:* very angry due to injustice **16** *appeal to sb.* (for sth.): make a request to sb. for sth. **23** *clump:* walk by putting down one’s feet heavily **27** *rutting stag:* brünftiger Hirsch **50** *approval:* act of saying that sth. is good **52** *marble:* Murmel

"You were?"

"Carrying that big plastic sack around and picking up everyone's garbage, and not saying anything, and whenever anyone laughed or made fun, you took no notice. You looked ..." Ana thought for a second, "... kind of dignified, I thought. You really did."

They were walking home. The school bus had dropped them off at the general store.

The sun felt warm on Declan's face. Declan carried only one book, *The Chrysalids*, which he had picked up in his English classroom because it looked interesting. By contrast, Ana's satchel was bulging with books.

"These books are heavy," said Ana.

"Is that a hint?" Declan took her satchel and slung it over his shoulder. "Here, you can bloody well carry mine." He handed her his book.

Ana laughed.

"What's so funny?"

"I was thinking about Thomas. Kate is annoyed at you for teaching him bad words."

"There was only one, and it wasn't so bad."

"You'll have to tell it in confession along with all your other sins," Ana said lightly.

"I don't go to confession. I've finished with all that."

Ana said, "I go at least once a month; I like it."

"I don't believe most of the blather the priests tell us anyway," said Declan. "All that codology about heaven and damnation, hellfire and eternal punishment. I believe it even less since ..." He stopped. "I don't think there are any punishments or rewards, but if there are, then they're here in this life, that's what I believe."

"I believe in heaven," said Ana. "Whenever I think of my real parents, I always think of them as being in heaven."

Declan said, "Real parents? What ..."

But he didn't have time to speak further. Thomas came to meet them as he often did, running in his slow, heavy way. The bus from his special school got home a little earlier most days. He called out their names, happy to see them, and rushed at Declan and wrestled him. Declan enjoyed his tussles with Thomas, who was surprisingly strong and courageous. They kept it up all the way to the house.

Later, Declan and Ana sat out on the porch in the sunshine.

Declan blurted out, “What did you mean about your *real* parents? I thought my uncle and aunt were your parents.”

“Huh?” Ana’s mouth fell open. “Matthew and Kate are not my parents – not my real ones, that is – I thought you knew that!”

Declan frowned. “How would I know if nobody told me?”

“They should have told you. Perhaps they thought you knew.”

“And you’re not my cousin?”

“Of course not!” Ana laughed.

“Then who in God’s name are you, then?” Declan felt a little angry. Why hadn’t they said? Was it possible they’d told him the day he arrived? Maybe his uncle had mentioned it when they were driving to Otter Harbour; he remembered very little of that first day.

“I’m an orphan,” said Ana, “same as you. Matthew and Kate took me in when my father was killed in a logging accident six years ago. I don’t remember my mother; she died when I was a baby.”

“And Thomas is not your brother?”

“No.”

“But why Matthew and Kate?”

“My father and Matthew worked together logging.” She pointed. “Over on the other side of the mountain.” Ana shrugged. “I had nobody else. Matthew just came for me, that’s all I know.”

“What about the eejit?”

“The what?”

“Thomas. The idiot. We call them eejits in Ireland.”

Ana flushed angrily. “That’s a terrible thing to call a person. And Thomas is not an idiot! He was born with Down’s syndrome! And he’s one of God’s children, just like you. And he’s wonderful and I love him. And Matthew and Kate love him, too. And if you think ...”

“Hold on there! I didn’t mean anything by it. I’m sorry. I like Thomas, too. You sure get mad over nothing.”

“I do not get mad over nothing. You’re so cruel sometimes. Thomas is ...” She clenched her fists as if about to strike him.

“Ana, I said I’m sorry. You’re right. But I don’t mean to be cruel. I’m sorry.” He put his arm around her shoulders but she shook it off.

▷ **5** *dignified:* impressive, worthy **10** *satchel:* small school bag · *bulge:* swell outwards **25** *blather:* foolish talk **26** *codology* (IrE infml): act of practising deception or lying **27** *eternal:* everlasting **37** *tussle* (infml): fight **40** *blurt sth. out:* say sth. suddenly, often tactlessly **52** *orphan* ['ɔːfn]: child that has lost his or her parents **58** *logging:* work of cutting down trees in the forest

"Look, what do you want? You want me on my knees begging for forgiveness?"

Ana was so upset, tears started in her eyes. "Declan, sometimes you're such a jerk! You make me …"

Declan glowered in silence.

"You get me so mad sometimes, I could … I could scream!"

Declan said nothing until she became a little calmer. Then he said, "So tell me about Thomas."

"Promise never to use that ugly word again."

"I promise."

"We love Thomas."

"Matthew and Kate adopted him, too, right?"

"It's the same story almost," said Ana. "Kate told me. He was left on the steps of the chapel. Nobody knows who his mother is."

Declan shook his head in disbelief.

"Father O'Connor was new in the parish then and didn't know what to do with a tiny, newborn baby wrapped in a blue blanket, so he asked the repairman, who happened to be there in the rectory fixing the plumbing, what he thought he should do, and Matthew – that's who it was of course – took a look at the baby and said it would be hard to find a home for a child who'd been touched by the fairies …"

"Touched by the fairies? Matthew said that?"

"According to Kate, yes. I had to ask what it meant. Anyway, Matthew took the baby home to Kate, and she called him Thomas after somebody-or-other, and now this is his home."

Declan frowned and shook his head again in disbelief. "I bet Miss Ritter's another one! Her house burned down, right?"

Ana nodded. "She lost everything she owned. She forgot to buy insurance. She had nowhere to go, and Matthew …"

"Matthew and Kate took her in," Declan finished for her. "They're both people-fixers! I knew it. That deal we made. They think they can fix me so I won't want to go back home. Well, Matthew and Kate Bloody Doyle are not going to fix me, let me tell you, not me, not Declan Doyle!" He flung himself from the porch and down to the yard. "I'm no TV set that needs fixing! I wasn't left on any chapel steps for those two phony interfering fixers to find me!"

"Declan!" cried Ana. "Where are you going?"

"That's my business!" he yelled back as he headed for the beach.

He stayed down on the beach, sitting on the rocks, until it was almost dark, his head a wild ravel of thoughts. Those meddling fixers had forced him to come to this foreign country. What right had they to make such a decision for him? Now they had talked him into making a deal with the intention of fixing him like the others – Ana and Thomas and Miss Ritter. Well, they would not trap him in their sly web with their clever smiles and coaxing ways. He would have no part of them and their world. So long as he didn't feel part of their world, he wasn't.

His uncle found him. "Kate has your dinner in the oven."

"I'm not hungry."

"Come on up anyway. The wind is cold."

"Leave me alone."

Matthew left him.

By the time Declan returned, Ana and Thomas had gone to bed, and he could see his aunt and uncle in the living room watching TV.

"Is that you, Declan?" called Kate.

"Good night." He did not stop, but, shivering with the cold, went straight up the stairs to his room.

▷ **4** *jerk* (sl): idiot **16** *parish:* area which has its own church and clergyman **22** *fairy:* Fee **37** *phony* (infml derog): false, fake **41** *meddle* (derog): interfere **46** *sly* (derog): clever in a deceitful, i.e. dishonest, way · *web:* Netz · *coax sb.:* persuade sb.

FOURTEEN

"Mind if I sit?"

Declan looked up from his lunch. It was Joe Iron Eagle. Declan's answer was to shift slightly to make more room.

Joe sat on the step beside him. The steps led down to the track and playing field, where a football game was in progress.

"That blonde girl with the sunglasses, she your sister?"

"Ana? Kind of a second cousin."

"Pretty."

"Hmmnn."

"You sign up for the science fair?"

"Science fair?"

"You weren't listening. There's to be a science fair in Sechelt. All the schools. Good prizes for original projects."

"What good prizes?"

"Books. Botany, zoology, physics, chemistry."

Declan snorted.

"I put your name in as my partner."

"You did? You must be crazy!"

"You game?"

"Maybe."

Silence.

"You sure you want me to be your partner?"

Joe grinned. The grin changed his face completely. It started slowly, wiping away the dark, brooding cast of his features, what Declan had initially taken to be meanness or toughness, and lit up his face so that it seemed at once innocent and mischievous. “You’re not as dumb as you look,” said Joe quietly. “We could win big.”

“Maybe.”

Joe grinned.

After awhile, he said, “So you pegged Dybinski.”

“That’s right.”

Joe reached into his lunch bag. They ate in silence, watching the game.

“Too bad,” said Joe after awhile.

“What’s too bad?”

“Too bad you had to peg Dybinski.”

“He had it coming.”

“Maybe. But he would’ve stopped bugging you. Eventually.”

“Eventually. In some dim and distant future,” said Declan sarcastically.

“Patience.”

“Huh?”

“Patience. It takes patience.”

“Yeah? Well, I guess I’m not a patient person.”

“No.”

They ate in silence. When they were finished, Declan got up. “See you later.”

“Sure.”

* * *

Declan killed a squirrel in the yard, and Ana was furious.

“It’s only an old gray squirrel,” said Declan, unable to understand why she was so upset.

“A squirrel is an animal, Declan. Just like us; we’re animals, too. Killing an animal for no reason like that, just to show how smart you are, is cruel. You gross me out! You really do! I just wish Matthew and

▷ **3** *shift:* move **10** *fair:* exhibition **16** *snort:* make a sound caused by forcing air through the nose with a loud noice in order to express impatience, disgust or contempt **19** *You game?*(sl): Do you want to do it? **24** *features:* Gesichtszüge **25** *initially:* at the beginning **27** *dumb* (infml): stupid **30** *peg sb.* (sl): defeat sb. in a fight **39** *dim and distant* (idm): (here) not soon **41** *patience:* ability to wait for sth. without complaining **49** *squirrel* ['skwɜːrəl; BE 'skwɪrəl]: Eichhörnchen **54** *You gross me out!* [grəʊs] (sl): You’re disgusting!

Kate had left you in Ireland, I really do! Then you could kill as much as you liked, and no one'd notice!"

Declan saw that even Thomas was unusually silent and grim. He watched Thomas sit down beside Ana on the front step, trying to comfort her by patting her gently on the shoulder and saying "There, there" over and over, the way he had probably heard Kate say it.

The incident had occurred when Declan was showing Thomas how to push several long nails through an apple so that the harmless fruit became a weapon. "We throw them at the Brits," Declan had explained, "the English soldiers." He drew back his arm. "Watch," he said and fired the apple at a squirrel that happened to be exploring the shade of the cedar hedge.

All children in the Falls Road were ace marksmen. Years of throwing stones at British soldiers had seen to that. Declan had developed this special skill when he was a member of the Holy Terrors, so it was no surprise to him when he scored a direct hit on the squirrel. One of the four-inch nails pierced the animal's small head and another penetrated the chest and killed it instantly. An excellent shot, Declan congratulated himself.

Thomas had picked up the dead squirrel and carried it into the house to show Ana. Declan heard Kate order Thomas outside with the dead animal.

Declan felt miserable about upsetting Ana once again and mulled it over when he was lying in bed that night, trying to understand why she had thought it cruel. He wasn't cruel. The thought upset him. How could it be cruel to kill an old squirrel? When they were learning how to harass the British, they'd practised on cats, and they had never considered their behavior cruel – necessary, but not cruel. Their practising on cats had helped to make them so deadly accurate that the Brits had to protect themselves behind plastic shields.

He lay with his head turned on the pillow, staring out the window. A full moon made the quiet night silvery and bright. It had been hard at first to get used to the quiet in this place. Living in Otter Harbour was almost like losing your hearing: no traffic noise; no yelling and screaming and banging of garbage can lids, which was what the women of Falls Road did whenever the British soldiers prowled their street; no whine of military armored vehicles constantly patrolling the neighborhood. Instead, there was the sound of the sea and the songs and cries of birds. Otter Harbour was another world. It was good to know that the house was safe, that he would not have to clamber into his jeans in the middle of the night because the Prods were about to burn the house down, or because the Brits were breaking in to terrorise them with one of their so-called security searches.

Declan's street had had three houses burned down last year when a bunch of Protestant militants stole a car from downtown and set it alight in the street beside the McLarens' house. The car exploded. The fire trucks came and were lucky to save the block. As well as the McLarens there were the Carneys and the Sullivans made homeless that night.

Declan had not been having his nightmare so much lately, but tonight, because he had been thinking about the car exploding in the street, it returned.

The nightmare started as it always started with the white wool sweater and a pale sun with no warmth in it shining fitfully through Belfast's toxic gloom and through the tea shop window onto Mairead's white sweater. Declan was outside the window of the tea shop. He could see his ma and his sister inside, drinking tea, smiling at each other. He hammered on the window trying to warn them, but they did not see or hear him. He yelled and screamed at them, but they went on drinking tea and smiling. He ran around the corner to the entrance, but the door was locked and he could not get in. He ran back to the window where they were sitting and he pulled off one of his shoes and pounded on the window with it, and just as they turned, surprised to see him there, the bomb exploded.

The nightmare now erupted into a thousand fragments of flying glass as the front of the tearoom blew out into the street. Which made no sense, for it had been a car bomb in the street that had caused the explosion. Declan was untouched by the blast, but everyone in the tearoom was blown up high into the sky. They began to fall to earth

▷ **7** *incident:* thing that happens **12** *cedar* [siːdər]: Zeder **13** *ace* (infml): excellent at sth. · *marksman:* person who can shoot accurately **15** *skill:* ability to do sth. very well **18** *penetrate sth.:* pierce through sth. **23–24** *mull sth. over:* think about sth. carefully **27** *harass sb.* [hə'ræs; BE 'hærəs] : trouble sb. continuously **35** *garbage can lids* (NAmE): the tops of dustbins **37** *whine:* sound made by a sirene **41** *clamber:* climb with hands and feet **56** *toxic:* poisonous **64** *pound:* beat **66** *erupt:* break out **69** *blast:* explosion

in slow motion. He ran around frantically among the falling debris, his face upturned to the smoke-filled sky, searching for his ma and his sister. If he could catch them, they would be safe, he thought. It was his duty to save them; he wanted to save them; he ached to save them. But he could not find them. His arms were stretched wide, ready to catch them, but he could not see properly with all the dust and smoke. Blood-soaked, once-white linen tablecloths floated to the pavement in terrible slow motion and settled over the bodies to become shrouds. He stumbled over something and fell to the ground. He put out his hand and saw a white wool sweater, now spattered with red, lying crushed on the pavement beside an unbroken porcelain teacup.

He woke up in a sweat as always. But this time he was not calling out. He lay there in the moonlit room, listening to the thump of his heart and the quiet music of the ocean, a whole world away from a porcelain teacup.

He remembered the squirrel. It made no sense, any of it. How could Ana and Thomas and Kate get so upset over the death of a rodent – that's all it was – when on the other side of the world they'd killed his sister and his ma, innocent people blown to pieces?

FIFTEEN

It was a calendar of birds and it hung on a nail over his uncle's rattan chair in the kitchen. Declan took it down and flipped through the pages. April was the month of the great blue heron. His ma and Mairead died in April.

September was a horned puffin, October a Canada goose, November a common loon, and December a bald eagle.

For Declan the December eagle was an omen, for hadn't it watched over him during his attempted escape to Sea Island? So it was only fitting that this eagle now guard that promise of freedom, that last day of December, which Declan had colored in red with a crayon so that when December came around and his Uncle Matthew glanced up at the calendar he would not fail to notice both the reminder of his promise and the eagle's fierce eyes and deadly beak threatening revenge should he and Kate renege on their promise.

Meanwhile, in the month of the puffin, Declan could stop running for awhile, he could relax; the deal with his uncle and aunt was forcing him to slow down and take things easy. He was surprised at the relief he felt: For the first time in five long months, he could stop rushing; he could stand still.

▷ **1** *frantically:* in extreme fear · *debris* [də'briː; BE 'debriː]: Trümmer **4** *ache to do sth.:* desperately want to do sth. **7** pavement (BE): Bürgersteig **9** *shroud:* cloth in which a dead person is wrapped for burial **18** *rodent:* Nagetier **21** *flip through sth:* turn over the pages, looking briefly at the contents **24** *puffin:* Papageientaucher **25** *loon:* Seetaucher · *bald eagle:* weißköpfiger Seeadler **32** *beak:* hard horny part of a bird's mouth **33** *renege on sth.* [rɪ'neɪg]: break sth. (esp. one's promise)

Five months ago, with the deaths of his ma and sister in April, he had suddenly become a different person – had changed overnight. Joining the Holy Terrors had allowed him to lose himself in action and revenge. Then when Matthew sent for him, giving the police a good reason to get rid of him, he had lived like a wild animal, constantly on the run, always looking over his shoulder.

Now he could stop searching for ways to escape. A few months in this peaceful place between the sea and the mountains would do him no harm, would help build up his energy and strength for his return after Christmas. And if those two meddling, do-gooder fixers, Matthew and Kate, thought they were going to work on him to change his mind, then they had another think coming. Declan felt almost lighthearted.

He thought about his return to Ireland. A new year. It would be a new, triumphant Declan keeping the promise he had made himself when he was torn away from his native soil: He said he would be back and he would. He felt tough, invincible. It would be a new beginning.

And once he was back, he would join the IRA if they would have him. Brendan Fogarty said they were recruiting for the Fianna, the IRA youth auxiliary for young people who were quick and smart, who knew the streets and the police and the Brits, who knew the ropes. Declan was already an expert maker of gasoline bombs. He knew just the right mix of sugar and flour and gas, and the right kind of bed-sheet strips that made good fuses. Milk bottles made the best bombs. He chuckled to himself as he remembered the joke about the woman who asked the milkman to leave her one bottle of milk and two empties.

And he knew how to make a nail bomb with gelignite and razors and nails and ball bearings, knew how to attack the Brits on foot patrol with fast hit-and-run tactics, knew how to steal a double-decker bus – as the Holy Terrors had done – and wedge it in one of the Shankill Road streets, set it on fire, and burn the Protestants down, the way they had burnt and destroyed the Catholics in the Falls and Ballymurphy neighborhoods.

He would make a good IRA man.

He would strike a blow for national liberation, a blow for Ireland's freedom.

And he would take revenge for the deaths of his sister and his parents.

At night as he lay in his Canadian bed, listening to the ocean, he thought often of his ma and his sister. He still found it hard to accept that they were dead. Gone. Death was so final. He remembered his ma in many different ways. Standing at the door of their house, Mairead only five, clinging to her legs, himself about eight, playing with the other kids in the street. "You've played enough, Declan. Don't you see it's dark?" Her voice worried. Or out in the street at four in the morning with all the other women, thumping and rattling their trash-can lids on the curbs, bravely refusing to be intimidated by the Brits or the police terrorising the Catholic neighborhood with their surprise search-and-harass games.

He began having his nightmare less often.

* * *

"Make that noise again."

"Hmmnn?"

"The birdcall. I like it."

Joe pursed his lips and whistled.

Declan laughed. "I can't tell the difference between your whistle and the real thing."

"Red-wing blackbird." Joe pointed to a bright flash of black and red in the thicket.

It was lunch hour. The small lake was a mere five minutes' walk from the school. Declan lay back in the grass, relaxed and happy, the warmth of the sun on his face.

Joe sat watching the lake, back straight, his legs folded under him.

"Too nice a day to waste in school," Declan murmured.

"You talk all the time of going home to Ireland," said Joe. "But you know what?"

"No, what?"

▷ **12** *have another think coming:* be forced to change one's ideas **17** *invincible:* too strong to become injured or defeated **20** *auxiliary:* person or thing that helps or supports **21** *know the ropes:* know the rules or procedures for sth. **24** *fuse:* Zündschnur **25** *chuckle:* laugh quietly **28** *gelignite* ['dʒelɪgnaɪt]: Gelantinedynamit · *razor:* Rasiermesser **29** *ball bearing:* Kugellager **31** *wedge:* pack tightly in between a space **44** *cling to sb./sth.:* hold on tightly to sb./sth. **48** *curb* (NAmE) = (BE) *kerb:* concrete edge of a pavement at the side of a road · *intimidate sb.:* frighten sb. **59** *thicket:* a lot of small trees growing closely together

"You will stay here. You like it too much to leave."

"Not a chance."

"I know it." Joe laughed. "You're hooked."

Declan opened one eye. "What do you say we take the afternoon off school?" Joe shook his head. "No thanks." "You scared you'll get into trouble?"

"No."

"Then why not?"

Joe grinned. "I like school."

"I'll fight you for it," said Declan. "I win, we skip school. You win, we go back, okay?"

"I don't fight," said Joe.

Silence.

"But I'll wrestle you, if you want."

"Wrestle?" said Declan.

Joe nodded. "No striking. Wrestling only."

"Okay." Declan leaped to his feet and crouched, ready to wrestle.

Joe stood calmly and pulled off his sweater and his shirt. He peeled off his sneakers and socks. Then he undid his belt and stepped out of his jeans, and stood practically naked in his Jockey shorts.

"You don't need to undress," said Declan, embarrassed and puzzled, glancing quickly around to see if Joe's performance was being observed.

Joe folded his clothing carefully and placed the pile on the ground beside an old cedar tree. "I don't like to look all mussed going back to school."

Declan laughed. "You think you're about to win?" He threw off his sweater.

"Of course." Joe grinned and rushed at Declan, grasping his smaller opponent in his arms and throwing him down quickly with a thump, pinning his shoulders to the ground.

Declan gasped as all the wind was knocked out of him. "I wasn't ready!" he choked.

Joe jumped up and stood back, grinning. "Best man is two falls. First fall goes to me." He crouched, waiting for Declan to rise.

Declan got up slowly, resting on one knee until he was breathing normally. Then he advanced cautiously, arms ready. They met. Declan tried to get a grip on Joe, but his fingers slid uselessly off his adversary's slick skin and hard-muscled body. Joe had no trouble, however, gripping Declan's shirt and pulling him off balance.

"Wait!" yelled Declan. "I want to take off my shirt."

Joe stood back, grinning. Declan wriggled out of his shirt and threw it to the ground, not taking his eyes off Joe, prepared should he rush again and try to take him by surprise. But Joe waited until Declan was crouching and ready, his bare skin pale and gleaming.

They met and grappled. Declan tried to get Joe off balance, but Joe was too quick on his feet, shifting and wriggling, using his strong grip and muscular arms to force Declan down. They fell together, wrapped around each other, pulling and pushing, grunting like a pair of wild animals. Joe tried a pin, but Declan arched his back and, kicking out at the sky with his legs, managed to pull himself clear. He spun about immediately and threw himself at Joe's dark shoulders, twisting himself, coming up on his knees behind Joe with a sweaty, sliding half nelson. But he couldn't hold it. Joe's neck muscles strained, his arms and shoulders bulged. Declan fell back with a gasp, and Joe was on him, and they rolled about in the grass for awhile, each trying to gain the advantage, until they were at the very edge of the lake, Declan on his back, too exhausted to hold Joe off. He could see a pair of mallards upside down as Joe pinned him for the second time. "You win!" he gasped.

Joe stood back, gasping for breath, his torso soaked with sweat.

Declan rose unsteadily to his feet. "You're the powerful wrestler, Joe, right enough." He grinned and reached for his shirt.

"Good fight," said Joe happily, as he dressed.

The mallards, a duck and a drake, clambered from the lake and stood watching the two boys.

"We'd better go to school," said Declan.

The shrill, piercing whistle of a red-wing came fluting up from the thicket as they started back.

▷ **3** *be hooked (on sth.)* (sl): like sth. very much so that one becomes dependent on it **10** *skip sth.* (infml): not attend or go to sth. **14** *wrestle* ['resl]: ringen **17** *crouch:* make oneself smaller by bending one's knees and back **22** *puzzled:* surprised **24** *pile:* several things lying one on the other **25** *mussed* (NAmE infml): disorderly **39** *adversary* ['ædvəseri; BE -səri]: opponent · *slick:* smooth and slippery **46** *grapple:* get hold of sb. and try to fight **49** *grunt:* make a sound like a pig **50** *pin:* attempt to hold sb. down · *arch:* bend **54** *half nelson:* wrestling hold **65** *mallard:* Stockente · *drake:* Erpel

* * *

At the end of October, Ana told him he had put on some weight. "You look healthier," she said one afternoon as they strolled home from school. "More relaxed."

Declan frowned and brushed the hair out of his eyes.

"But you need to smile. And laugh. Leah says you're not so stuck-up the way you used to be."

"I was never stuck-up," Declan declared hotly. "And as for smiling and laughing, I leave that to those who have reason to."

"She thinks you're cute."

"Where I come from cute means cunning. Like a fox."

"She means lovable."

"Is that right now? And what did you tell her?"

"Me?" Ana shrugged nonchalantly. "Oh, I just told her to keep her eyes off my big brother."

Declan almost smiled.

The month of the Canada goose was a good month for sunshine. The trees were changing color and there was a hint of fall in the air as Declan and Ana set off for school each morning.

Although Declan had earned a grudging respect from the other kids at school, he knew they did not like him. He could read it in their too-polite faces, but he did not care: They were no countrymen of his. Joe was different, of course. Declan's friendship with him was growing stronger each day.

Most of the teachers did not take to him either, Declan noticed. Though his natural curiosity led him to read most of the required texts, he handed in no work. He didn't care what they thought of him.

Mr. Hemsley, however, who taught social studies and who was young and cheerful, tried to encourage him.

"Your test scores are very good, Declan, especially in the essay questions. I admire a student with opinions of his own." He smiled. "Try to keep an open mind, though, and try to understand other points of view, okay?"

Miss Oliver, the elderly English teacher, wanted to know why he had handed in no essays. "You cannot hope to pass the course on test marks alone," she said. "You're an intelligent boy; why do you take no part in the class discussions?"

"I've nothing to say," lied Declan, not revealing the real reason, which was that participation spelled acceptance, and he had no intention of accepting any part of this alien country. That would be falling for his aunt and uncle's trap; he wasn't that much of a fool.

The weather stayed warm right into November, month of the loon, and then became suddenly, sharply cold. Otter Harbour blazed an autumn bronze, and the huge old maples on the main street flared crimson against the sea and the sky and the dark embrace of the forest.

▷ **10** *cunning:* clever **13** *nonchalant:* casual, not showing any interest **17** *fall* (NAmE): autumn **19** *grudging:* unwilling **25** *curiosity:* being eager to learn new things **37** *reveal:* show, allow to be seen **43** *maple:* Ahornbaum · *flare:* burn brightly **44** *crimson:* very deep red

SIXTEEN

It is midnight and the wind and the ocean are restless and he too is restless in his bed, unable to sleep.

He remembers.

It is Thursday, April 16. The day before Good Friday. Their last day.

He sees them clearly in his memory, recalls their faces on that fateful morning, their expressions, their gestures, and he searches now for some sign in their faces and voices of their doom. But there is none.

Mairead is excited, of course, because today is her birthday, and she is trying on her new white wool sweater, a gift from her mother. It is 7:45 in the morning and the three of them are in the kitchen. Mary Doyle is cooking breakfast and a man on Radio Ulster is singing "Have I Told You Lately that I Love You?" He sings it "luurv."

Mairead is happy. She tells her ma that she *luurvs* her sweater – it fits perfectly, and she *luurvs* her ma, and she *luurvs* her big brother, and she thanks Declan again for the beautiful notebook that is large and heavy and has blank, creamy pages, enough for a whole year, and which is just perfect because Mairead loves to write, and someday, she always tells them, she will be a famous poet like William Butler Yeats.

She admired the notebook in Marks and Spencer some weeks earlier. "It would make a perfect diary, too," she said. Declan checked the price and made a quick calculation; he would be able to afford it if he was careful with his pocket money. It had a picture on the cover of a beautiful Victorian lady seated at a desk writing. "It's so elegant," Mairead said, as she stroked its cover with her fingers.

She is a skinny kid with long, long legs, who walks daintily with her back straight; she has brown hair and lively blue eyes. She takes after her ma. Declan is supposed to take after his da. The new sweater helps fill her out a little and looks good on her. "Take it off while you eat your breakfast," says their ma, so she peels it off carefully over her head and suddenly she's skinny again in a faded pink T-shirt that says Make Love Not War. She folds the sweater neatly and carries it into the living room and places it on the back of the sofa for later.

Breakfast is fried eggs and refried boiled potatoes from last night's dinner and toast and marmalade with hot milky tea. Mairead likes tea whenever her ma lets her have it, but mostly she drinks milk. Declan is old enough to choose whatever he wants. He is reading a science-fiction book while he eats his breakfast.

Their ma opens the kitchen window and throws out a handful of crumbs for the birds. Then she sits down with her tea and toast. She takes Declan's book away from him. "Manners at the table, Declan. I swear to heaven you'll be reading in your grave."

Declan, remembering, ransacks the memory, listens and watches his ma keenly. But despite "grave," there is no inkling of death in either her voice or her manner. She is relaxed and happy on her daughter's birthday, looking forward to their outing in the city. She sips her tea, her elbow cupped in her hand, the hot teacup near her pale cheek, her blue eyes drowsy and fond.

The initial excitement of her birthday gifts over, Mairead is now dreamy. She sips at her glass of milk and gazes over her mother's head out the kitchen window at a pair of spring sparrows on the sandstone window ledge pecking jerkily at the bread crumbs. Ten is an important birthday. She had three birthday cards, one each from Declan and her ma, and one from her friend Rosaleen.

▷ **4** *Good Friday:* the Friday before easter **6** *fateful:* decisive, causing everything unpleasant that happens thereafter **7** *doom:* terrible fate; death **19–20** *William Butler Yeats* (1856–1939): Irish poet and dramatist **21** *Marks and Spencer:* British department store chain **25** *Victorian lady:* lady from the Victorian Age (1819–1901) **26** *stroke sth.:* touch sth. tenderly **27** *skinny* (infml): very thin · *dainty:* neat, pretty **28–29** *take after sb.:* resemble one's mother or father in many ways **32** *fade:* lose colour **41** *crumb:* very small piece of bread or cake that has fallen off a larger piece **42** *manners:* social behaviour **44** *ransack sth.* ['- -]: search (for) sth. thoroughly **45** *keen:* eager, intense · *inkling:* hint **49** *drowsy:* sleepy · *fond:* loving **52** *sparrow:* Spatz

There is not a sign of doubt or foreboding on her dreamy young face, not a hint in her happiness that today is the day she must die.

Declan, still remembering, sees himself finish his breakfast and get up from the table. He watches himself run up the stairs and brush his teeth, then grab his lunch off the kitchen table where his ma has left it for him, kiss his ma and Mairead hurriedly, unthinkingly, absent-mindedly, thinking only of Tim O'Malley waiting for him, ready for school, unaware that this is the last time he will ever see his ma and Mairead alive.

Several hours later he is summoned to the headmaster's study, and the headmaster is nodding at him. His old, serious face, the creases around his mouth as he speaks the words. The policeman is standing beside the head-master's desk. Help? Who can help? Death is a scythe that cuts you down.

He walks home. The house is empty. Everything is tidy and in its place, just the way they left it before they went off on their birthday jaunt. His eyes search for a message, a note, some final word scribbled by his ma, but there is nothing. The kitchen counter is neat: the toaster with its bright daisy-yellow cover, the teapot with its blue wool cap, cleaned and rinsed, the brown plastic dish rack emptied of its knives and forks and plates. There are still a few crumbs left outside the window from the sparrows.

He sits on the old sofa bed in the living room and stares at his ma's pictures of Pope John XXIII and the Sacred Heart hanging on the wall, Jesus with his long, sad, suffering face, left hand pointing to his burning heart, a prayer in the lower margin: "Come to Me, all ye who are heavily burdened and I will give you rest."

Mrs. O'Malley from next door comes in. "Are you there, Declan, love?" And when she sees him sitting there, his school bag still clutched in his hand, she says, "Oh sweet Jesus – they killed your ma and the child!" And starts crying and sits beside him and clutches him to her shoulder, weeping hot tears into his hair.

Father Coughlan, the parish priest, is next. He tiptoes into the house and makes the sign of the cross and takes Declan's hands into his own. "God be with you, boy, in your time of trouble." And he blesses him and tells him he must be strong and does he wish for him to send Mrs. Maloney from the rectory to stay in the house with him for a week or so while he telephones his uncle, Matthew Doyle, in

Canada? Declan is staring at the Sacred Heart. He shakes his head. He will be all right; Mrs. O'Malley will be coming in.

When he gets rid of everyone, he locks the door and climbs the stairs. He opens his ma's bedroom door and stands there just looking. On the wall over the bed is another Sacred Heart picture. Suffering. The room is very empty. Then he goes to Mairead's room, which is his own room also, divided in two by a curtain strung up on a pair of wall hooks – the house, like all the others in the row, has only two bedrooms. The diary he gave her for her birthday is on the hurriedly made bed. There is a pair of soiled white socks on the floor beside the bed. Her green blazer, part of her school uniform, hangs on the back of a chair. He picks up the diary and stares at the Victorian lady on the cover.

He goes to his own side of the room and lies on his bed and stares at the ceiling, the diary clasped in his hand, and he waits in silence. He is waiting for them to come home, rattling and laughing through the door downstairs, tired and happy after their day in the city, waiting for them to dismiss this empty, tomblike silence.

But they don't come.

The funeral is on Monday. The IRA with their black berets and dark glasses make a political thing of it. The police are there in full force. The Brits, too, in their armored six-wheeled Saracens. If they try anything, there will be a riot for sure. Schools are closed. All the victims. All the mourners. Hundreds attend. The coffins closed.

It is the last he ever sees of his ma and his sister, two dark wooden boxes, one of them small, on the shoulders of the IRA pallbearers. He watches, his face pale in the cold spring sun. The pain he feels is unbearable, but he wants to guard it and nourish it so it will grow, and when it has grown powerful enough it will explode.

He watches the coffins being lowered into the consecrated ground.

▷ **1** *foreboding:* knowledge or sign that danger or trouble is coming **6–7** *absentminded:* thinking of other things **10** *summon sb. (to sb./sth.):* ask sb. to go to sb./sth. **14** *scythe* [saɪð]: Sense **17** *jaunt:* short journey, made for pleasure **20** *rinse sth.:* wash sth. **30** *clutch sth.:* hold sth. tightly **37** *rectory:* house in which a priest lives **46** *hook:* Haken **54** *rattle:* make short sharp sounds quickly **56** *tomb* [tuːm]: small building into which the dead are laid **58** *funeral:* religious service for the dead **60** *Saracen:* type of armoured vehicle **64** *pallbearer:* person who walks beside or carries a coffin at a funeral **66** *unbearable:* that cannot be endured · *nourish sth.:* keep sth. alive **68** *consecrated:* holy

He doesn't cry.

The Brits don't try anything. There is no riot. Not this time.

After the funeral he holds it in for two days at the O'Malleys'. All day and night and the next day. Then the next night, he climbs through the window into his own empty house and sits on his ma's bed and weeps, weeps until he thinks it will kill him.

He stops remembering.

The wind keens in from the black Canadian sea and rattles his window. He pushes himself up out of bed and looks out at the dark night and the turbulent sea.

He remembers again that picture of his mother's – the Sacred Heart, that sad, suffering Jesus face on the wall.

It looks a lot like his Uncle Matthew.

SEVENTEEN

Matthew sat in the garage cleaning a rifle.

"Looks like an antique," said Declan. "Did you bring it with you when you ran away from Ireland?" He watched Matthew carefully as he said this. Always, no matter how much he tried to needle his uncle, Matthew never got angry. Now, however, Declan was delighted to see a rictus of irritation jerk at his uncle's mouth.

Matthew paused to collect himself. Then he looked up. "It's a First World War rifle," he said evenly. "Ross 303.

Made here in Canada."

Declan watched him. The man was a coward; why else would he put up with Declan's taunts and insults?

"You ever fire a rifle?" said Matthew.

"No."

"You like to try?"

"Maybe." He'd love to fire a rifle, but he wasn't about to let his uncle know that.

Matthew closed one eye and peered down the inside of the rifle barrel. "No time like the present." He got up. Declan followed him out along the cliff and down over the rocks to the beach, where his uncle set up a soda pop can on a rock. He loaded the rifle, pushing in five cartridges at the top, and handed it to Declan.

▷ **6** *weep:* cry heavily **8** *keen in:* (here) sound like a cry of sorrow **14** *rifle:* Gewehr **17** *needle sb.* (infml): provoke sb. **19** *rictus:* act of opening one's mouth because of surprise, disgust, etc. **24** *taunt:* provocation **33** *soda pop* (NAmE): fizzy drink made with flavoured soda-water **34** *cartridge* (BE) = (NAmE) *shell:* Patrone, Kartusche

The rifle was heavier than it looked. Declan lifted it to his shoulder, closed one eye, and sighted along the barrel. He pulled the trigger and was surprised at the punch it gave his shoulder as the gun exploded.

"I missed." He was annoyed with himself. He wanted to show his uncle he could do it.

"Pull the stock hard into your shoulder. When you're ready to fire, take a good breath, let it out, and squeeze the trigger. Squeeze, don't pull – like this." He showed him. "Try again."

The second shot struck the rock underneath the target.

"Squeeze gently. Take your time."

Declan rested his cheek on the polished stock and took careful aim. The third shot nicked the edge of the can and sent it spinning and rattling from its perch. Declan's blood tingled with the power of the rifle; his heart swelled. How he would love to have in his sights the dirty Prods who'd killed his family!

Matthew propped the target back up.

Declan's fourth shot blew the can away. He thought his heart would burst.

"You'll do," said his uncle.

* * *

When Kate discovered that Matthew had been teaching Declan to shoot, she was very angry. She was so angry that she forgot Declan was there. Hands on hips, eyes blazing, she said to her husband, "Is this why we brought the boy all the way from the madness of Northern Ireland? To teach him gun shooting? Is that it?" She thrust out her jaw.

"Now, Juno," said Matthew, trying to calm her down, "the gun puts meat on the table ..."

"Don't Juno me, you peacock! I'd rather starve than eat meat gunned down by any child of mine! I never thought I'd see the day that Matthew Doyle would be putting a gun in the hands of a child!"

"... after all, Kate, a man must learn to survive in this ..."

"Man, is it? And him only ..."

"He'll soon be a man, isn't that the truth, Declan?"

But Declan had already gone, creeping up the stairs to – his room, a smile on his face, leaving his uncle to survive Kate's wrath on his own.

* * *

They set off before dawn, driving the truck up the narrow mountain road in the darkness.

After an hour they parked and set off on foot in the gray light. Matthew carried the rifle and binoculars, Declan the water and food in a small pack on his back.

The woods were cold and deep.

The higher they climbed, the colder it became. "Deer like the rocky ridges below the summit," said Matthew. "The snow forces them down to the lower slopes. Once we're up above the tree line, we can track them back down."

Declan had never hunted before, except for Brits, he thought, grinning to himself, and he would never admit to his uncle how much he was enjoying the gradual climb through the thin pines and mountain alder, the huckleberry and salal bush. He breathed deeply, pulling the cold air into his lungs, exulting in the strength of his legs.

They emerged from the forest and scrub and rested on the ridge, drinking from their water bottles. The sky behind them was pink. Declan looked out over the seemingly endless forest at the dark sea half a mile below.

Matthew pointed down. "Otter Harbour."

Declan stared. From up here the village was tiny. Ana and Thomas and Kate were shrunk to invisibility.

His uncle searched the forest through his binoculars for signs of deer. Declan watched an eagle soaring overhead, its feathered pinions outspread, white head pinked by the dawn.

Matthew passed the binoculars to Declan and pointed to a spot below them under the ridge. "Two blacktail does," he whispered.

Declan looked through the glasses. At first he could see nothing; everything was a pinky gray. Then something moved, the flick of an ear. The deer's head came up from its feeding. It was looking around.

▷ **2** *barrel:* Lauf **3** *punch:* strike, blow **6** *stock:* Schaft **13** *perch:* place where a thing is placed · *tingle:* prickle **16** *prop sth. up:* place sth. so that it stands up **28** *peacock:* Pfau **35** *wrath* [ræθ; BE rɒθ] (fml): very strong anger **43** *deer:* Rotwild **44** *ridge:* area of narrow flat land on a mountain · *summit:* highest point of a mountain **50** *huckleberry:* Heidelbeere **51** *exult in sth.* (fml): get great pleasure from sth. **52** *scrub:* land covered with underdeveloped trees and bushes **58** *shrink – shrank – shrunk:* become smaller **61** *pinion* (fml): wing **63** *doe:* female deer

A second deer raised its head above the salal. The two deer were very far away.

"We're downwind," whispered Matthew. "They haven't seen us. Follow me."

They moved slowly, stalking the deer. Declan copied his uncle, walking softly for several paces, stopping to look and listen, then moving down toward the clearing. Soon they were less than a hundred yards away. Declan could see them quite clearly without the binoculars. A third deer had joined the other two. Tall and stately with wide antlers, it held its head high, gazing around with large ark eyes while the other two browsed. Must be a buck, thought Declan.

Matthew bit his lip as he pushed the worm bolt of the rifle forward. It made a barely audible click. Declan saw the buck jerk his head toward them, eyes staring, ears alert, nose in the air. They waited silently. The buck moved slowly to a new position. Matthew passed the rifle to Declan. "The buck," he whispered. "Aim just below the shoulder."

Declan felt a thrill. His uncle was trusting him to shoot this magnificent buck! He rested the well-worn stock on his hand, the polished wood running the whole length of the barrel. He pulled the butt into his shoulder and fingered the trigger. His heart pounded with excitement. He had to force himself to breathe slowly. Calm down, he told himself. As he sighted along the barrel, he could feel the blood tingling in his fingers.

The buck was an easy target. Declan could see the full length of the animal's powerful body and the fine head with its high antlers. The buck stepped forward slowly and gracefully on his long legs, head straight. Then it bent its head to browse. Declan had him in his sights at a spot just under the shoulder. His finger tightened on the trigger. Remember to squeeze, he told himself. Take your time. And then he saw – long legs – his sister, Mairead walking to school on her long legs, straight, with her shoulders held back, just under the shoulder, remember to squeeze, brown hair, white neck, birthday, she didn't know she was to die that day, that morning, death was forever, death was for keeps, deer about to die, not knowing, white sweater stained with blood, explosion, death, long legs. Declan took a deep breath. He was sweating. All he had to do was squeeze the trigger and the 303 bullet, faster than sound, would blow a hole in the deer heart and the helpless animal would never hear the sound of the shot.

A blue jay gave its harsh cry.

The buck's head jerked up, ears twitching. He gave a snort. The two does bounded away in long graceful leaps.

"Now!" said Matthew.

But still Declan did not pull the trigger, and then it was too late. The buck leaped and was gone.

He had waited too long. Declan stared at the place where it had been. He lowered the rifle and released the bolt.

The sun came up over the top of the mountain and reached its bright fingers down the slope toward them.

Declan could feel it warm on his neck. He handed the rifle to Matthew. "Sorry," he said. "I should have got him." He felt miserable. What had got into him? What would his uncle think of him now? He said, "I don't know what came over me."

His uncle smiled.

Declan stared at the sight of a smiling Matthew. If he hadn't known better, he would have thought his uncle was happy.

"Let's go," said Matthew. "We can try to track him down the mountain."

They set off, moving down the slope after the buck, but though they stalked the deer trails and searched the deadfalls through their binoculars for over two hours, they did not catch another sight of deer.

They ate and rested and listened to the chatter of squirrels and the songs of birds, and Declan turned his face to the sun and heaved a huge sigh of contentment.

Matthew, too, seemed contented. He lay back when he'd finished his sandwich and closed his eyes.

After awhile, Matthew, his eyes still closed, said, "One side is as bad as the other."

"Hmm?"

▷ **5** *stalk:* walk carefully in order to hunt sth. **7** *clearing:* open space without trees within a forest **9** *stately:* imposing **10** *antlers:* Geweih · *gaze:* look steadily **11** *browse:* feed by biting off tiny pieces of grass · *buck:* Hirschbock **12** *bolt:* Schloss **13** *audible:* that can be heard **18** *trust sb.:* have confidence in sb. **40** *jay:* Eichelhäher **41** *twitch:* sudden rapid movement of a muscle **47** *release sb./sth.:* remove sb./sth. from a fixed position **60** *deadfall:* Baumfalle **64** *heave sth.:* (here) utter sth. **65** *contentment:* state of being satisfied

"The war in the North. One side is as bad as the other." Declan sat up with a jerk. "What are you talking about?"

Matthew opened his eyes. "Declan, violence, killing, it solves nothing ..."

"Let's get back," said Declan.

They got up and headed back along the edge of the mountain toward the truck. When they had been walking for an hour, they stopped for a rest. Declan's legs were tired now and his body ached. They sat on a log and drank from their water bottles.

Then suddenly, Matthew dropped his bottle and snatched the rifle from the log where he had leaned it. Declan's heart lurched. Without pausing, his uncle pushed the rifle bolt home with a metallic rattle, pulled the rifle into his shoulder, and raised the muzzle high over his head.

Declan looked up. A cougar was crouching on the limb of a tree fifteen feet above their heads. Its thick tail twitched and its ears stood up high on its small head as it stared down at them.

Matthew kept the rifle pointed at the cougar. "Freeze!" he grunted to Declan.

Declan set his jaw. He eyed the honey-colored cat. It was as long as a man, with heavy, powerful hindquarters. "Shoot!" Declan hissed at his uncle. "Shoot!"

Matthew held his fire.

The cougar's shoulders bunched. To Declan it looked as though the powerful animal was about to leap. He could not tear his eyes away from its pale green eyes. He yelled at the cat and waved his arms. "Aaarrgh!" he growled. "Aaaarrrgh!"

The cougar took one last look at them, then turned quickly away, leaping from the tree into the salal and out of sight.

Matthew lowered his rifle. "That was dangerous, Declan. I said to freeze."

Declan said, "I scared him away. Why didn't you shoot? We could have been killed! A wild animal like that!" His heart pounded.

Matthew said nothing. He released the bolt of the rifle and picked up his water bottle. He pushed the bottle into Declan's shoulder pack and set off along the trail.

Declan followed. "Why didn't you kill it?"

"No need. Be different maybe if he'd been forced down by the snow and was starving. But there's plenty of game about. I would have had to shoot if he'd jumped."

"He scared the life out of me! I thought he was going to jump."

"He wasn't about to jump," said Matthew.

"How do you know?"

"You can usually tell. His ears were up. He was just curious – never seen Irishmen before. When a cougar's hunting, his ears lie back against the head."

"So you didn't shoot him because of his ears."

"That's right."

Declan looked sideways at his uncle. He sure was hard to figure out. Because he never rose to any of Declan's taunts about being a traitor who ran away from Ireland, Declan had concluded his uncle was a coward. But now he wasn't so sure: If he'd been in his uncle's socks, pointing a loaded rifle at a cougar, he would have fired for certain. Matthew had stayed pretty cool.

They continued along the trail. Declan felt weary.

It took an hour. He could have cried out for joy when he finally saw Matthew's old truck standing waiting for them. They climbed in. Matthew started the engine. "Want a mint?" Declan took one. They drove down the mountain in silence.

▷ **9** *log* [lɔːg; BE lɒg]: tree-trunk **10** *snatch sth.:* grab sth. **11** *lurch:* beat unsteadily **13** *muzzle:* open end of a firearm **15** *cougar* ['kuːgər] (NAmE): Puma **18** *freeze!:* don't move! **39** *game:* wild animals or birds to be hunted

EIGHTEEN

Tell me about Belfast, said Ana.

They were sitting out on the porch, wearing warm jackets. The month of the loon was a rainy one, cold and damp. Declan liked to sit and watch the different moods of the sea and the sky. Ana and Thomas sometimes sat with him.

"Where I lived, all the Catholics have a picture of the pope on the wall," said Declan, "like the one Matthew and Kate have." He went on to describe the Falls Road area, where many of the women painted the sidewalks outside their homes orange and white and green, the colors of the Irish flag. The Protestants did the same on theirs, only they painted the Union Jack, red, white, and blue. And the Protestants hung English flags out of their windows.

The graffiti on the gable ends of the houses said things like: IRELAND FOR THE IRISH; KILL KILL KILL; BRITS OUT; BLOOD DEBTS REPAID IN BLOOD; and (painted by the Prods during the night) KILL THE POPE.

Derelict houses, bricked-up windows, rusty corrugated tin, bleak streets, barricades of brick and barbed wire, the air hazy with the smoke from coal and turf fires, no grass or greenery, broken pavement and guttering, starving dogs roaming about. While Radio Ulster played constant country-and-western music, the smell of poverty clung to everything like cigarette smoke.

"Declan, it sounds awful. Surely the rest of Ireland is not like that?"

"No. Ireland is beautiful. We live in one of the poorest parts of Northern Ireland."

"You must have hated it."

"Not really. We're used to it. My ma worked in the shirt factory. We got by. But compared to the nicer parts of Belfast, the houses in my neighborhood are pretty awful."

There were rats. They left hard pellets on the kitchen counter. His ma took care of the baiting and setting of the traps, though the rats were usually cunning enough to avoid them. If the traps ever killed, then Declan did not know of it, for his ma was always the first up in the morning, and she never spoke of it.

Afterward, after the bomb, when he was alone in the house; he set a trap and awoke one night to the sound of thumping. He thought it was the Brits or the Prods breaking in. Heart racing, he pulled on his jeans and tiptoed down the stairs. The noise, a constant rhythmic sound of something being thumped against the counter tiles, was louder. When he saw what it was, he backed off. Then he slipped his hand into his ma's oven mitt and gingerly picked up the trap and dropped it into the backyard toilet and waited until it had drowned. Then he threw it into the bin, trap and all.

"I hate rats," said Ana.

"I hate them, too," said Declan, "but there's worse things in Belfast than rats."

"I'm glad I live here," said Ana.

Declan did not reply, but he thought about the Belfast he had just described to Ana and then he thought about the day on the mountain hunting with Matthew. The eagles, the jays, the graceful deer, the quiet, pine-scented air.

"What are you thinking about?"

Declan brushed back his hair. "How people in different parts of the world can lead such totally different lives."

Declan knew he wasn't telling Ana the complete truth about his thoughts. What he'd said was true as far as it went, but also at the back of his mind was a blister of a thought, a nagging suggestion that his

▷ **13** *gable:* Giebel **17** *corrugated:* wrinkled · *bleak:* gloomy, depressing **18** *barbed wire:* Stacheldraht · *hazy:* misty **20** *guttering:* Abflussrinnen **22** *cling to sb./sth. – clang – clung:* hold on to sb./sth. **29** *get by* (infml): manage to survive **31** *pellet:* very small ball **32** *bait:* food to trap and catch an animal with **37** *thumping:* heavy knocking or beating **42** *oven mitt:* heat resistant glove that covers four fingers together and the thumb seperately · *gingerly:* very carefully **58** *blister:* Blase · *nag sb.:* worry sb.

day in the woods with his uncle had been only a part of Matthew's larger plan in his role as Chief Fixer. Matthew and Kate were trying to drag Declan into their world, and he refused to be dragged. Such tactics by his uncle and aunt only strengthened his resolve to return to his home; he would show them that Declan Doyle was made of much tougher stuff than they'd bargained for.

* * *

"Keep the books, Joe, you earned them."

"I wouldn't have got a second in the juniors without you, Declan."

"Sure you would."

"Wrestle you for them!"

"Some other time, Joe. Ana's waiting by the bus. See you tomorrow."

When Declan and Ana got off the bus, they turned into the lane. Declan noticed Thomas run and hide in the cedar hedge.

"Pretend we didn't see him," said Declan.

They went in the back door of the house. "Where's Thomas?" said Declan in a voice loud enough for Thomas to hear. They came back out into the yard. "Where's Thomas?" shouted Declan.

"I hope we haven't lost him!" cried Ana.

"Oh no!" cried Declan, pretending to become quite upset. "Thomas, Thomas! Where are you? Come back to us, Thomas."

A muffled giggle came from under the hedge.

"Did I hear something?" said Declan hopefully.

"It was only the cry of a lonely blue jay in the branches of the Douglas fir," said Ana, declaiming, storybook fashion.

"No!" said Declan, enjoying himself and following Ana's tone. "It sounded to me like the tortured cry of a poor boy imprisoned in the deep deep earth."

"It was a bird, I tell you."

"You're wrong, Ana. It's poor Thomas trapped under the deep earth." Declan made loud sniffing noises. "I can smell the orange he had for his lunch."

"The smell you smell is the cedar hedge, sharp like lemons," said Ana in her storybook voice.

"He's here, I tell you!" shouted Declan. "And we've got to save him before it's too late!"

Louder giggles from the hedge.

"I hear him! I hear him!" Declan bent down. "I see him. Ana! I see him! It's Thomas! He's trapped in the earth under the hedge. Help me free poor Thomas from his prison!"

Thomas giggled and squirmed as they dragged him out. They stood him on his feet. Thomas screamed with laughter, pleased with himself for having fooled them for so long. "I trapped, Declan. I trapped … deep … deep."

Declan and Ana threw their arms around him. "What a fright you gave us, Thomas!" said Ana.

"We thought we'd lost you!" cried Declan.

That night as he lay in his bed, head turned to look out the window at the night sky, Declan remembered how happy he had felt when they were playing with Thomas, dragging him out from under the cedar hedge, and his mind fixed uncomfortably on the word *dragging*. The Fixers, Matthew and Kate, were intent on dragging Declan into their world. Ana and Thomas were a part of that world. He would miss Ana and Thomas, he realised.

The realisation was like a weight around his heart.

* * *

Miss Ritter came down to the wind-battered porch one evening to watch a storm over the ocean, and when she saw them all gathered there, she said brightly, "How nice you could come."

Kate made room for her on the broken sofa. "Sit here, Miss Ritter, and I'll bring you a cup of tea. There's a pot made fresh only a minute ago." She got up and went inside.

"Good evening, Matthew," said Miss Ritter. She looked about her, smiling. "Ana." She nodded. "Thomas." She nodded again. She came to Declan and frowned slightly. "Oh!" She appeared surprised. "I thought you emigrated to Australia, Walter!"

"This is Declan," said Ana.

"Oh, how silly of me. But he looks so much like Walter when he …"

Kate handed Miss Ritter her cup of tea.

▷ **22** *muffled:* not heard clearly **25** *Douglas fir:* Douglastanne · *declaim:* speak like an actor on a stage **41** *squirm:* wriggle **56** *wind-battered:* badly shaped because of frequent and heavy wind

"Thank you, dear," said Miss Ritter, taking the cup and saucer in her birdlike hands.

Kate sat down beside her.

"It's so good of you all to come," said Miss Ritter. "I get a little nervous sitting indoors during a storm. It's so much nicer when friends come to visit." She kept darting glances at Declan. "I was born in this house …" She looked at Declan expectantly. "Lived here all my life," she finished uncertainly.

Declan nodded solemnly.

"I never moved." Miss Ritter stared at Declan, and when he said nothing she nodded her head several times, took a sip of tea, and gazed out over the sea, a bright smile on her face.

Matthew and Kate were talking quietly together; Declan couldn't hear what they were saying. He looked over at Ana. She smiled at him and shrugged her shoulders as if to say, "Relax. Poor old Miss Ritter is like this sometimes."

In easy silence they watched the sky diminish to darkness. The storm blew high, crashing breakers up onto the rocks, and the lightning flashed on the far horizon.

* * *

The morning after the storm, they found a harbor seal pup on the beach.

"It's dead," said Declan after examining it.

"You can't be sure," said Ana. "It could be unconscious.

"Consh …" said Thomas.

They sat on the beach and watched the pup.

"It shivered," said Ana. "I saw its nose shiver. It's alive."

"Leave it to die," said Declan. "It's almost dead anyway."

"Matthew and Kate will fix it," said Ana. "They fix animals all the time. They fixed a Canada goose that had something wrong with its wing, and a baby raccoon we found at the bottom of Headley Cliff, and …"

"Hmmph!" Declan kicked the sand. "The Fixers strike again!"

Ana and Thomas climbed back up to the house and got Matthew to come down.

Declan watched him squatting, examining the animal without touching it. "Its mother could be out searching for food. Best not to touch it."

"But what if it lost its mother in the storm?" said Ana.

"Leave it for an hour," said Matthew. "If its ma isn't back by then, well ..."

They returned to the house and watched through binoculars for an hour. The mother did not come. The seal did not move.

They hiked down to the beach with Matthew and stared at the pup.

"It will die if we don't do something," said Ana.

"Then leave it die in peace," said Declan.

"We could leave it to die, right enough," said Matthew, nodding his head.

Ana said, "No! We should try to save it!"

Thomas became excited and started jumping about. "Save it!" he cried. "Save it!"

Matthew nodded. "There's always the chance it might live if we take it." He looked at Declan.

Declan shrugged and turned away. He wanted no part of it. Matthew would never make a Fixer out of him.

"We could try," said Matthew. He bent and rolled the pup onto his forearms, and, clasping it to his chest, carried it up the cliff to the house.

▷ **6** *dart:* move quickly and suddenly **9** *solemn:* serious **17** *diminish:* become less **20** *seal pup:* Seehundbaby **26** *shiver:* tremble from cold, fear or shock **35** *squat* [skwɑːt; BE skwɒt]: sit on one's heels or on the ground with knees drawn very closely to the body **43** *hike:* walk **55** *bend – bent – bent:* lean down

NINETEEN

For Declan the days were dissolving into one another, one following another, it seemed to him, seamlessly. Otter Harbour was a quiet, unhurried place, so to Declan the days seemed all the same.

Early on Sunday morning, before anyone else was up, he decided to take a look at Matthew's workshop to check on the seal pup, which had now been there two days. The seal, motionless on a bed of straw in a big cardboard box near the heater, regarded him with a milky eye. Matthew should have let it die on the beach. The seal was too far gone: it was beyond Matthew's ability to fix it. Declan couldn't help a brief feeling of satisfaction. The Fixer would fail. The seal would die.

He wandered down to the shore to sit and watch the ocean and the gulls from a high rocky promontory a short distance from the house. He came to this wild place often when he sought isolation. Somehow, the sight of the sea beating and frothing against the rocks made him feel at home, at the center of things, even though his home was far away; the wild hiss and draw of the surf somehow calmed him.

Today, however, there was another figure on the beach near the rocks. When he got closer he could see it was his Aunt Kate. She was sketching with pastel crayons. A large pad of sketch paper rested on her knees.

"I didn't know you were an artist," said Declan.

She smiled up at him. Again, he was reminded of his ma; they had the same eyes, the same easy, fond way of smiling. "I've always painted," she said. "Ever since I was a child." She tilted the seascape sketch so he could see.

Declan studied the dark sweeping colors on the page. Then he looked at the scene before them. “Is that what you see?”

“Today, it’s what I see.”

“You did the paintings in the house,” said Declan. “I can see that now.”

“I paint from some of the pastel sketches, yes. There’s a small gallery in Sechelt owned by a woman from Dublin, Moira Donaghue, who came out here about the same time we did. Moira started taking some of my stuff a few years ago. Then a gallery in Vancouver wanted some. So they keep me busy.” She sighed happily. “Ah! Every day is different here. It’s the grand country. I try to catch the different moods of the sea and the sky.”

Declan laughed. “I was only thinking how every day is the same, one day after another with nothing to tell them apart.”

Kate said, “You’re dead wrong, Declan, so you are. Each day is unique – one of a kind.” She pointed. “The clouds are never the same; they move constantly, changing their shapes. The light is always different at different times of the day and the year. I like the early-morning light best; it’s purer somehow, have you noticed?”

Declan shrugged.

Kate said, “Life is change. Clouds, light.” She looked at him slyly. “People, too; they grow and change.”

Declan said nothing to that. He remembered: Kate was a Fixer, too, just like Matthew.

* * *

“What kind of a name is Iron Eagle, anyway?”

“A First Nation name.”

What does that mean?”

I’m a native Indian. When I was baptized, I was given a Christian name – Joe Summers. But many First Nation people take the old names now.”

▷ **2** *seamless:* without a dividing line **7** *cardboard:* very thick paper used to make boxes **12** *promontory* ['prɒmәntɔːri; BE -tri]: Vorgebirge **14** *froth* [frɔːθ; BE frɒθ]: cause to foam **16** *hiss:* sound like a long ‘s’ · *surf:* waves breaking on the seashore **19** *sketch sth.:* draw sth. quickly without details · *crayon* ['kreɪɒn]: Wachsstift **26** *sweeping:* stretching over a large area **53** *baptize sb.:* jdn. taufen

They were eating their lunches on the outdoor steps. The playing field was empty, but several runners were circling the track in the afternoon sunshine.

"I don't see many of your people at school," said Declan.

Joe shrugged. "They leave to hunt or fish. Some go logging."

"Why not you?"

"I stay."

"Yes, but why?"

Joe often frowned over a question and took his time answering. He did so now. Declan waited.

"I stay because I want an education," he said at last "I plan to study law."

"A lawyer." The tone of Declan's voice conveyed his low opinion of law and lawyers. "I thought you wanted to be a scientist."

Joe shook his head. "I want to help my people." He saw the puzzlement on Declan's face and laughed. Then he became serious again. "Like many of my people, I live on a reservation" He waved his arm in a wide sweep over the distant forest. "Once, all this land, as far as an eagle can see, belonged to us. It was ours to hunt and fish. But it was taken away from us. We have been fighting for many years to get it back."

Declan's eyes shone with interest. "Fighting?"

Joe nodded. "The government men listen to us and say they will do something. But they never do."

"What kind of fighting?" said Declan, remembering the Indian pictures of his childhood, feathered headdresses , bows and arrows.

"We demonstrate. We close the roads through our land. We fight in the courts."

Declan snorted. "Fat lot of good that kind of fighting will do!"

"One day we will win. Justice will be done."

"Justice!" Declan laughed. "You think the government will give you back your land?"

"Perhaps not all we ask. But some. Enough to make our spirits strong again."

"So that's what you meant by patience! You'll need plenty of it. In my country, we fight for what we're entitled to. We don't wait for someone to hand us what is ours. We fight to drive the English out of Ireland."

"I know. I've seen pictures of Ulster, and I've seen how you kill each other."

"Oh, have you, now!" said Declan angrily. "Well, first of all, we call it the North of Ireland, or the Six Counties. Only the Prods call it Ulster, because England has six of the nine counties of the true Ulster. Second, the IRA is fighting for justice, too! But they don't have your so-called patience – I call it cowardice – to wait another hundred years for the English to give us what is ours!"

Joe crushed his lunch bag in a quivering fist and stood up. "You are calling me a coward?"

Declan stood to face him, glaring.

The school bell rang. It was the end of the lunch period.

Declan sighed. "No, Joe. I didn't mean to call you that."

* * *

November was gone. The kitchen calendar turned at last to the wild stare of the eagle, and now the crayoned square, December 31, stood out as a crimson promise of freedom. Declan felt strong. Only one more month and he would be home!

Matthew asked Declan to help him with the fishing early one morning when the gulls were flocking offshore over the herring shoals.

There was only room for two in the boat. "Who usually goes out with you?" said Declan.

"Ana. She's a good fisherman. Sometimes I go alone."

Matthew rowed the boat and showed Declan how to use the herring rake, a long, thin pole of sharp bristling nails, by sweeping it down into the water beside the boat and lifting it high, full of wriggling herring. They filled three buckets to the brim with herring in less than fifteen minutes.

"Why do you need so many herring?" said Declan.

"Bait for salmon." Matthew sat down and pulled on the oars. "And I thought I might try some on the seal pup. Mash 'em up. We've been feeding it milk and vitamins, but there's not much improvement so far."

▷ **13** *lawyer:* Anwalt/Anwältin **36** *entitle sb. to sth.:* have the right to have or own sth. **47** *quiver:* tremble **57** *flock:* gather at one place **58** *shoal:* large number of fish **63** *rake:* Harke **65** *brim:* top edge **69** *mash sth.:* crush sth. to make it soft

Declan said nothing.

Matthew stopped rowing to show Declan how to place the hooks and lower a line for the salmon that were feeding underneath the shoal.

There was no wind. Declan's jeans were covered in herring scales, his hands and sleeves, too. He sat upright in the prow, holding the rod in two hands, waiting for a coho salmon to strike his herring bait. And when it did, his heart leaped with the salmon.

When they got back with their catch, Ana said, "Declan caught the coho?"

Matthew almost smiled. "He's not bad."

Ana grinned at Declan and winked.

* * *

Kate invented a special formula, which they fed three times a day to the seal pup. Ana called it a fish shake. Kate mixed herring, water, milk powder, vitamins, and cod-liver oil in the blender. Declan became interested and began to enjoy helping with the feeding. He could not rid himself, however, of the thought that he was participating as another "Fixer," and this always bothered him.

Kate poured some of the formula into a baby bottle, but the pup refused to drink it, pulling its head away and wailing like a baby. Matthew hit on the idea of pushing a plastic tube down its throat while Declan, Thomas, and Ana held its head and Matthew poured the fish shake a few drops at a time down the tube. Declan noticed that the pup's body was warm; why did he expect it to be cold? he wondered.

After a week, the pup became used to the tube, swallowing it hungrily, and they were able to increase the amount of food.

Ana was delighted. "It's going to live!" she said to Declan. "I knew we could save it."

"We save it!" cried Thomas, excited.

"I wouldn't have given twopence for its chances," admitted Declan.

"What shall we call it?" said Ana. "We can't keep saying *it;* it should have a name."

"Is it a girl or a boy seal?" said Declan.

Ana had to admit she didn't know. "We'll ask Matthew."

Matthew said he thought it was a boy. "What about Harper Harbour Seal," suggested Declan, "Harper for short." Thomas giggled. "Harper! Harper!" "Harper it is," said Ana.

▷ **6** *rod:* thin, straight piece of wood **7** *coho salmon:* Pacific salmon **15** *cod-liver oil:* Lebertran · *blender:* Mixer

TWENTY

Declan and Joe stood on the clamshell beach near the mouth of the river. Behind them, houses of weathered cedar straggled in random array along the river bench. Smoked and dried salmon hung on racks under orange tarpaulin shelters. Behind Joe's village, snow-capped mountains reared high above the dark line of fir and spruce.

Joe pointed toward the river mouth where it emptied into the sea. "Do you see? The far side of the sandbar."

Declan looked. He saw a ridge of rocks near the far shore, but that was all.

Joe laughed. "You will see when we get closer. Get in." He waited until Declan was kneeling in the front of the canoe, then he pushed off and leaped in. "Grab your paddle."

The current was weak. They paddled past the sandbar to the middle of the river, where the current grew stronger and stronger until the canoe was moving swiftly toward the river mouth. Joe steered in the direction of the rocks.

Declan stared ahead, his heart racing with excitement. Now he could see it, a narrow corridor of white water boiling through two walls of rock. Declan swore silently. He was a fool to have listened to Joe. They would never make it through that narrow channel in a canoe! The frail craft would break into a thousand pieces, and they would be thrown into the churning river and hurled against the sharp black rocks.

They moved closer. "Paddle!" Joe screamed over the roar of the torrent. Declan paddled. The nose of the canoe swung straight. They were in the dark corridor. The canoe leaped and bucked in the frothing foam like a frightened horse. Declan was terrified. The walls of rock on both sides were but inches away. He could see daylight ahead where the rock walls ended, but they would never make it. Joe was screaming something, but Declan, deafened by the roar of the river, soaked by the spray, and certain he was about to die, could think only of his drowned, battered body being swept out to sea, never to be found.

The front of the canoe lurched up, then down, scraped the side of the rock, lurched again, and catapulted out of the foaming crevice into the wide river mouth. They were through! The noise was behind them now. The canoe slowed as the river joined with the sea.

Declan turned. Joe was laughing. "Wasn't that ... wasn't that ... wild!"

Declan could not speak. His heart was like a drum in his chest.

Joe let out a whoop of joy.

They turned and paddled back in the slow-moving current near the village shore.

* * *

Ana had an important part in the school Christmas play. "Last year we did *A Christmas Carol*," she said to them all one evening.

"You were the Ghost of Christmas Past," said Kate. "I helped Ana make the costume," she explained to Declan.

Ana said, "This year we're doing *Amahl and the Night Visitors*."

"Ah, yes, the story of the little crippled boy," said Kate. "We saw it in Dublin one time, remember, Matthew? The year Mountbatten was killed by a bomb, and his young grandson, and another boy?"

Matthew looked up from his book. "Nineteen-seventy-nine. The same year we saw the pope. The first time a pope ever visited Ireland."

▷ **1** *clamshell:* Muschelschale **2** *weather sth.:* change in appearance due to the weather · *straggle:* spread out in an irregular way · *random:* done without purpose **3** *array:* order, arrangement **4** *tarpaulin:* waterproof protection sheet **5** *rear:* rise high · *spruce:* Rottanne **14** *current:* Strömung **19** *swear – swore – sworn:* curse **21** *frail:* weak, fragile · *craft:* boat **22** *churn:* move about violently **25** *torrent* ['tɔːrənt; BE 'tɒr-]: violently rushing stream of water **30** *deafened:* unable to hear **32** *drown:* die in the water because one is unable to breathe **35** *crevice:* narrow opening in a rock or wall **45** *A Christmas Carol:* Christmas story by Charles Dickens (1812–1870) **48** *Amahl and the Night Visitors:* Christmas opera by Gian Carlo Menotti (born 1911)

"Ah, the pope was lovely," said Kate with a sigh. "I'll never forget him. 'On my knees I beg of you to turn away from the paths of violence' he said."

Matthew frowned. "In those words?"

"Those very words," said Kate. She turned to Declan. "A third of Ireland's population turned out to see him in Dublin at Phoenix Park. Ah! The excitement! We saw him again in Drogheda and followed him to Galway. The Galway racetrack, of all places! Matthew and I shivering in our sleeping bags all Saturday night behind the paddock. Then Sunday morning, you never saw so many people in one place in all your life! And the fine day for it. Your ma couldn't come because of the baby." She laughed. "You, Declan! You were that baby! It was almost October, and you only the wee thing. Ah! The lovely baby you were!" To Matthew, she said, "I can't believe it's thirteen years gone since! But it was all lovely' every bit ..."

"Kate!" said Ana impatiently.

"We're ready, child. Aren't we all waiting for ye?" She appealed to Matthew and Declan, who grinned, but said nothing.

"It's an opera in one act," said Ana as she gave them each a copy of the libretto. "I have the part of the mother. It's a big part. So I need ..."

"It's lovely you getting the part of the mother," said Kate, "but I'm not surprised one bit; you sing like a nightingale, doesn't she, Matthew, doesn't Ana sing like a nightingale?"

"... I need ..." said Ana.

"She does, right enough," agreed Matthew, nodding.

"I need you all to help me learn it. Declan, you are the crippled boy. Your name is Amahl. You hop about on a crutch. Matthew, you're Melchior, one of the wise kings – would you please put your book away? Kate, you're the second wise king, Balthazar – could you please stop thinking about the pope? Thomas, you're the third wise king. Your name is Kaspar and you're quite deaf, so mostly you sing 'Eh?' whenever anyone sings anything to you. Don't worry; I'll give you a sign."

Thomas looked confused. While Ana continued giving instructions to Matthew and Declan, Kate took Thomas aside and patiently explained to him what he was expected to do. When she was finished, Thomas was grinning happily. "Eh! Eh! Eh!" he said.

"Not yet, Thomas," said Ana. "Ready, everyone? Now don't forget to sing your part when it comes your turn. Don't worry about how it sounds."

"Who sings the parts of the shepherds who watch their flocks by night?" asked Declan, who had been looking ahead in his libretto.

"Mr. Hetherington has a special chorus of shepherds, but we could all do it together," said Ana.

Kate played the piano. They began unsteadily, amid much laughter, but once over the first couple of pages, became caught up in the story. Whenever there was the slightest pause in the singing, Thomas rushed in with his "Eh? Eh? Eh?" which added to the noisy confusion.

Kate had a good voice and sang confidently as she led on the piano.

Matthew sounded like a foghorn.

Declan was not altogether sure he liked being a crippled boy.

Finally, they reached the end of the opera. Amahl left his home to join the three wise kings on their journey to the Christ child in Bethlehem and they all sang together the shepherd's hymn of peace.

Kate said, "Ah! That was lovely, so it was."

Ana gave orders for a regular practice every evening after dinner.

* * *

Matthew had scavenged a child's discarded swimming pool for Harper's swimming needs, but the pup had come along so well after several weeks of fish shakes that Matthew thought he might now be ready to return to the sea.

"He doesn't look quite ready to me," said Ana. "What do you say, Declan?" She smiled her slightly tilted smile and gave him a wink.

Declan shook his head at Matthew. "Needs another week or two, I'd say." He knew how attached Ana had become to the pup, and if he

▷ **7–8** *Drogheda, Galway:* towns in the Republic of Ireland **9** *paddock:* small field on which horses are kept **13** *wee* (IrE infml): very small **25** *nod:* quickly move one's head down and up again to show agreement **26** *crippled:* behindert **27** *crutch:* stick that supports a crippled person when he or she is walking **41** *shepherd* ['ʃepəd]: person who takes care of sheep · *flock* (n): group of sheep **45** *amid* (fml): together with **59** *scavenge sth.* ['skævɪndʒ]: search through sth. for an item that can be used · *discard sth.:* throw sth. away

were honest, he would have to admit he was now fond of him, too; Harper had become a pet, splashing his tail and flippers in the water and barking with excitement whenever he saw them coming to play with him.

Matthew said, “You think so? Then it might be a good idea to feed him some live fish.”

Ana agreed. “Then he’ll know what to eat when he goes back home to the sea. Good idea, Matthew.”

So Harper stayed with them a while longer, his fish shakes now supplemented with live herring from the bait tanks at Pender. Ana could not bear to feed the live fish to Harper, so Declan had to do it while she watched. “What a pity one animal must die so another can live,” she said. “God sure created a strange world.”

“You’re right, Ana. None of it makes sense. Sometimes I think God is crazy.”

Ana said, “Bite your tongue!”

“No worse than you saying He’s strange!”

“I didn’t say God is strange. All I meant was, who says a seal is more important than a herring? Huh? They’re both animals, they’re both alive, right? Look at the way we kill and eat animals! Who says a human is more important than a pig or a calf or a lamb?”

Harper gobbled the herrings enthusiastically one after another, his shiny nose and whiskers reaching for the next even before the last had been swallowed.

“Well, Harper has no worries about the question,” said Declan, emptying the last of the bucket into the happy pup’s wide-open mouth.

* * *

Whenever Ana had to stay at school and rehearse for the school play, Kate asked Declan if he wouldn’t mind staying to walk Ana home along the dark road.

Ana wanted to take his arm. “Makes me feel like a real sister,” she explained.

“You’re not my sister, Ana. You’re not even my cousin.” He kept his arm straight so she couldn’t hold on to it.

Ana was quiet for awhile; then she recovered and chattered about some of the funny rehearsal mistakes: John Basinger, who played the part of the page and whose duty it was to carry the train of each of the wise kings as they entered Amahl's humble cottage, had pulled too hard on Kaspar's train, and Kent Niamin, who played the part of Kaspar and whose mother's heavy brocade curtain material was pinned uncertainly around his thin hips, was left standing in his Jockey shorts.

Declan laughed.

"You must have been totally bored watching us all make fools of ourselves," said Ana.

"I liked watching you," Declan admitted.

"All those shepherds falling over one another. The script just says 'shepherds' without saying how many. Mr. Hetherington put in two whole classes of kids from grades four and five so he could get more people involved. What a scream. But they sound good, don't they, the shepherds?"

Declan had liked the shepherds. "I liked the shepherds."

"And you liked me, too?"

He had hardly taken his eyes off her. "I liked you the best."

"Thanks."

Then Declan asked Ana what she wanted to be.

"When I grow up, you mean? I haven't thought about it too much. But working with animals would be interesting; a vet maybe?"

They walked along in silence. Then Ana said, "I'm afraid to ask you the same question, Declan."

"Why?" But he knew what she was thinking.

"I'm just afraid you'll start on again about joining the IRA and setting Ireland free from the English and all that stuff ..."

"It's not stuff!"

"Okay, sorry, but I can't stand it. I don't want to think of your being killed before your life really starts. My heart goes cold."

Declan was silent. She sounded a lot like Mairead sometimes. He took her hand. It was like ice.

* * *

▷ **10** *supplement sth. (with sth.)* ['sʌplɪmənt]: add sth. to sth. else **22** *gobble sth.:* eat sth. fast **28** *rehearse:* practise for a performance **37** *page:* boy attendant of a person of high rank · *train:* part of a long dress or robe that the wearer drags behind him **38** *humble:* poor **58** *vet* (infml) = veterinary surgeon: doctor for animals

Another evening, after rehearsal.

"You're very gloomy and silent. What is it? Didn't you like the way the rehearsal went?"

"It isn't that," said Ana.

"What, then?"

"I was just thinking."

Silence.

"I was thinking that I wish you weren't leaving us. I really do."

TWENTY ONE

It was time for the seal to leave.

They carried Harper down to the sea in a tarpaulin. He had put on plenty of healthy weight. Declan and Kate held the tarpaulin on one side, Matthew and Ana the other. Thomas guarded the front so their burden would not tumble off as they climbed down over the rocks.

Harper's black eyes glittered with excitement as he raised his nose in the air, smelling the sea. They talked to him like a baby.

When they got to the ocean's edge, they lowered Harper to the sand and stood back, watching him trundle forward eagerly, head swaying, into the waves.

"Good-bye, Harper," Ana called.

"Goo'bye, Harper," Thomas cried.

Kate said, "Ah! It's good to see him go back where he belongs. He'll be happier now. Home is where the heart is, after all."

They stood watching for several minutes as Harper dived and sported in the waves. After a while, the seal hobbled back up onto the sand, barking, wanting to play.

"Leave him be," said Matthew walking away toward the house. The others followed.

Harper started after them, but stopped when they kept going.

They watched the seal from the porch, looking down over the edge of the cliff at the dark, lonely figure on the beach. Declan could not take his eyes off the seal. "Go home, Harper," he whispered.

▷ **14** *glitter:* shine brightly **17** *trundle:* move heavily **18** *sway:* move slowly from one side to the other **23** *dive:* go under water **24** *hobble:* walk with difficulty

"Will he go away?" said Thomas.

"Soon," said Declan.

Harper plunged into the waves. He wasn't playing now.

"He's swimming!" yelled Thomas.

Matthew and Kate came out on the porch to watch. Matthew had his binoculars.

Harper swam boldly out to sea. All Declan could see was his shiny black head bobbing in the waves. The head got smaller and smaller. After awhile, he could not see it. He stared at the empty sea and felt a surprising, jolting sense of loss.

Harper had gone home.

* * *

After school on Friday, Kate told Declan and Ana, "Dinner is early today, and then Matthew and I are away shopping in Sechelt. The shops are open till nine." She pulled down the stove door and peered inside.

"Take me and Leah, too," said Ana. "We want to see *Beethoven*. It's a movie."

"Ah, Beethoven, is it?" said Kate. "I love the Ninth Symphony, so I do." She slammed the stove door shut.

"Not that Beethoven," said Ana, laughing. "This is a *dog* called Beethoven."

"But who's to look after Thomas?" said Kate. "Unless you take him with you, but come to think of it, there isn't enough room for all of you in the truck."

"Declan, would you look after Thomas?" said Ana.

"Sure," said Declan.

"Thanks," said Ana. "That's settled. I'll go call Leah."

"Ah, Thomas is no trouble, Declan," said Kate. "He likes the television, and when it's time for bed, he loves you to sit him in your lap and read him a story."

"So I've noticed. But if he sits in my lap, he'll crush me to death."

"Never the bit," said Kate, laughing fondly. Her face grew serious. "But he needs to be watched. I wouldn't want him to be fiddling about with the stove or playing with knives. Don't let him out of your sight for long, you understand? We should all be back by nine-thirty."

Declan nodded. "We'll watch TV together."

Which is what they did, and at eight o'clock, Thomas handed Declan a picture book. "Read me, Declan."

Declan took the book. *See You Later, Alligator.* He started to read. Thomas stopped him and parked himself on Declan's lap. He weighed a ton. Declan started the story again. The telephone rang in the kitchen. Thomas jumped up and ran for it. "I'll answer!" shouted Declan. Thomas picked up the phone and handed it to him.

"That you, Matthew?" Gruff voice.

"Matthew is out. Who's calling?"

"Joel Murphy, bartender at the Victoria. You must be Declan."

"Right."

"Is Kate there?"

"She's out, too."

"Will they be back soon?"

"Nine-thirty or so."

"Phew! That's too late. Look, Declan, Daisy Ritter is drunk as a fish. She's done this before. Right now – can you hear her? – she's singing her heart out."

Declan listened. It certainly sounded noisy there. He could hear a high voice singing "Darling Clementine." It couldn't possibly be gentle, ladylike Miss Ritter singing in the bar, he decided. "You sure it's Miss Ritter?"

"Do I know my own mother? Pretty soon she's gonna pass out. Last time she broke her collarbone. Ask Matthew. You think you could come down and fetch her? We tried already to take her home, but she started yellin' an' screamin' an' cuttin' up so bad we had to back off for fear of hurtin' the old lady. You think you could get over here and talk her down offa the pool table?"

"She's on the pool table?"

"You got it, Declan."

"I don't know if it'll do much good, but I'll be over."

"Make it quick, Declan."

Declan put down the phone. "Shoes on, Thomas. We have to go out. Get your jacket. Let's make it quick."

▷ **8** *bob:* move quickly up and down **10** *jolting* (fig): surprising **32** *never the bit:* of course not **33** *fiddle about with sth.:* play carelessly **44** *gruff:* rough **59** *pass out:* lose consciousness **60** *collarbone:* Schlüsselbein **62** *cut up* (NAmE): behave badly **63** *back off* (NAmE): give up **64** *offa* (sl): off the

"Where, Declan?" Thomas pulled on his sneakers.

"The hotel. Hurry." He helped Thomas tie his laces.

Declan had never been in a Canadian bar before. It was crowded, noisy, and smoky. He felt out of place as soon as he walked in with Thomas. Mostly men, they stopped what they were doing to watch Declan and Thomas make their way through the tables to the bar. Declan could hear a woman singing, but there was no sign of Miss Ritter.

"You Joel Murphy?" Declan asked the big, heavy man behind the bar.

"Thanks for comin', Declan." Joel Murphy pointed to an alcove at the back of the room.

It was Miss Ritter, all right. There was no mistaking the old lady's birdlike frame and gray hair. Standing daintily in the middle of the pool table and singing at the top of her voice about a bicycle built for two, she was surrounded by a crowd of people singing merrily along with her. In her hand she held a glass of liquor. She appeared to be enjoying herself.

Thomas laughed. "Miss Ritter!"

Joel Murphy took them over. Declan stood looking up at her. Miss Ritter saw him and stopped singing. "Walter!" she said.

"Hello, Miss Ritter," said Declan.

"And Thomas!" said Miss Ritter.

"We've come to escort you home," said Declan.

"Home?" Miss Ritter looked puzzled. Then she smiled. "Escort me, Walter?"

"That's right," said Declan.

Like a queen, the old lady held out her arm. Declan reached up and took it. Joel Murphy took her other arm. They lowered her gently to the floor.

"Thank you, Walter."

Joel stepped back. Declan and Thomas led her through the bar and out the door to the street.

It was dark and cold outside. Miss Ritter looked up at Declan. "Your Aunt Daisy has had a little too much to drink, Walter." She shivered.

Declan pulled off his sweater and slipped it over Miss Ritter's head. They walked her home. "I'm half crazy," sang Miss Ritter softly, "all for the love of you."

Declan took her upstairs to her room. "Thank you, Walter, for escorting me," said Miss Ritter. "You're very much like your father, you know. You were always a tender-hearted boy. Goo' night, Walter."

"Good night, Aunt Daisy," said Declan.

Later, while Matthew drove Leah home, Declan told Kate and Ana about Miss Ritter. "Ah, thank God she's home safe then," said Kate. "She fractured her clavicle last year when she took a fall after a drink, the poor thing. I'll go up to see if she's all right."

As he lay in his bed that night, Declan thought about Miss Ritter. Why had he gone to the hotel? Joel Murphy was an old worrier. Miss Ritter would have been all right until Matthew or Kate got there, wouldn't she? Why had he felt so protective toward the old lady? Why had he called her Aunt Daisy? There was something about the whole incident that bothered him. He twisted and turned in his bed for almost an hour, sleep eluding him.

Then just as he was beginning to settle down, a thought struck him. "No!" he wailed. He sat up. "They're making a bloody Fixer out of me!" he said aloud.

* * *

The gymnasium was decorated with red and green streamers; a huge PEACE ON EARTH. GOODWILL TOWARD ALL MEN sign hung over the stage.

The curtain went up ten minutes late, but by then everyone had settled down and an excited buzz of anticipation ran through the crowd.

Mrs. Gaynor, the music teacher, played the piano, and the children sang and acted their parts in the story of the poor crippled shepherd boy who makes a gift of his only possession – his crutch – to the Christ child.

After the conclusion of the opera, the entire cast came back on stage to sing "Silent Night," "Adeste Fidelis," and "Away in a Manger." The audience applauded.

▷ **2** *lace:* Schnürsenkel **11** *alcove:* Nische **46** *fracture sth.:* break sth. · *clavicle:* collar-bone **54** *elude:* escape, avoid **58** *streamer:* long, narrow ribbon of coloured paper **66** *possession:* property **68** *conclusion:* end · *cast:* all the actors in a play

When the singers finally came out of their dressing room, Ana a kid once again in sweatshirt and jeans and no longer an impoverished widow, Kate was the first to hug her. “Ah, you’re the lovely girl.” She kissed her. “With the voice of an angel.”

Matthew was next. “You make us all proud, Ana,” he said. He kissed her.

Thomas was next. “Proud, Ana,” he said happily, hugging her. Ana kissed him affectionately on the check.

Declan stood watching her excited face. “Did you enjoy it, Declan?” said Ana.

“I did,” he said.

They drove home, Declan and Thomas in the back of the truck blowing their breath on their hands to keep them warm.

“Well, it’s glad I am that the rehearsing is all over,” said Matthew when they were home. “A wise king I would never make. Maybe now I can go back to my reading.”

* * *

Ana and Thomas were excited about Christmas. Declan was excited, too, but for quite a different reason: He would be going home as soon as it was over.

He was on his way down the stairs one morning, when he overheard Kate say to Matthew in the family room, “It hangs over the house like a thick black cloud, so it does.” He paused on the stair, listening.

Matthew said, “Hmmph!”

Kate said, “There isn’t the one of us looking forward to Christmas this year, and that’s the truth.”

Declan guessed they were talking about him. He did not want to listen, but his feet wouldn’t move.

Matthew said “Hmmph!” again.

“Yesterday morning,” continued Kate, “Ana wanted to tear down that calendar of yours off the wall. Why? I says to her. ‘It’s that awful red square,’ she says. ‘I hate it!’ I looked at the eagle there on the wall and I’d swear to God if the creature hasn’t the evil eye.”

“Nonsense,” said Matthew.

"Nonsense yourself," said Kate. "Look at the rascal, will you? Fixing us with his cruel stare. Ana is right to want it down. 'Declan is leaving!' it seems to be screeching at us like a banshee."

Matthew said, "Hmmph!"

Kate said, "It mocks us."

Declan could listen to no more. He made a noise on the stair and entered the room just as Matthew was pulling the calendar down off the wall and stuffing it away out of sight in one of the kitchen drawers.

▷ **2** *impoverished:* poor **35** *rascal* ['ræskl; BE rɑːskl]: Schurke **37** *banshee* (IrE): female spirit with a special wail, thought to warn of death in a house **39** *mock sb.:* make fun of sb.

TWENTY TWO

Well, you better believe it, Joe.

"I was sure you would stay. I never took you for a fool, Declan."

"You don't understand. I've got to go back."

Joe was silent. Then he said, "I'll miss your ugly face.

"I'll miss your ugly face, too, Joe."

"You want to wrestle? See whose face is the ugliest?"

Declan smiled. "No thanks."

"You are like a brother to me, Declan."

Declan flushed with embarrassment. "You're not about to suggest we become blood brothers, I hope, Joe."

Joe grinned. "No. That's for the movies. But we could shake hands as brothers."

They shook hands.

* * *

Isn't it too cold for you to be sitting out here in the wind?"

"Ah, I have my warm jacket. And my mitts." Kate held up the hand that wasn't holding the crayon, leaving her elbow to hold down the pad on her knees.

"All the same ..." Declan sat down on a barnacle-covered rock and pulled the collar of his jacket up around his neck. "Will it stop you working if I sit a minute?"

"Not the bit." Kate did not look at him. She was watching the curl of the waves as they crashed on the rocks. "You looking forward to Christmas?"

"I don't care about any of that stuff."

"This will be our eleventh here in Canada." She gave him a quick glance. "Best thing we ever did was to leave Northern Ireland."

"Couldn't you have gone somewhere else – in Ireland, I mean?"

"Ah, the work was bad everywhere. In 1981 you could have a letter of introduction from the Holy Ghost and still find no work." The wind blew her hair. "That was the terrible year, 1981, the year your sister was born, and your da ..."

"My da was butchered by the dirty Prods!"

Kate put down her crayon. "Declan ..." She stopped.

Declan waited for her to go on, but she picked out another pastel and looked out to sea.

"It was the same year Bobby Sands of the IRA was elected member of Parliament, and him in the Maze prison on a hunger strike against the British. Less than a month later he was dead. Sixty-six days without the bit of food. There were terrible riots for more than a week in Derry and Belfast. Then they stopped, but broke out again, and this time they spread to Dublin." Kate shook her head. "The English sent six hundred more soldiers, making twelve hundred troops in the North. And more tanks. The fighting was terrible fierce. I never want to see the like of it ever again." Kate resumed sketching. "You were a child of three, Declan." She smiled.

"What was my ma like then, in those days?"

"Your ma was always the lovely woman, God bless her! She'd give you her last penny if you needed it. But with the death of your da, and then the new baby coming ... your poor ma was worried to distraction. Matthew had a friend who came out here, making good money in the logging, and he said there was plenty of work. We asked your ma to come with us, but she wouldn't. 'I'll not leave the place where I was born and where Liam is buried, and drag two children halfway across the world,' she said."

Declan tried to imagine Matthew and Kate leaving Ireland and leaving his ma and Declan and Mairead behind. How would things have turned out if his ma had gone with them? Would they be alive today? Instead of lying in the cold ground of Milltown Cemetery?

▷ **17** *pad:* sheets of paper fastened together at one edge **18** *barnacle:* Entenmuschel **32** *butcher sb.:* kill sb. brutally **34** *pastel:* crayon made from coloured chalk **43** *fierce:* brutal **44** *resume sth.* [rɪ'zu:m] (fml): continue doing sth. after having stopped **49–50** *to distraction* (idm): almost to a state of madness

Declan stood. "I'm chilled with the cold." He turned to go.

Kate packed her things. "I'll walk back with you. The light is gone, and the wind is stronger."

They walked home together into the wind on the strip of sand between the sea and the rocks.

* * *

It rained on Christmas day.

Thomas burst into Declan's room and woke him up. "Merry Christmas, Declan!" he cried, his eyes wide with excitement.

Declan opened one eye and looked out the window at the rain. Then he looked at the clock by his bed: six. He groaned and pulled the covers over his head. "Go away, Thomas. Let me sleep."

But Thomas would not let him sleep; he pulled at the covers until Declan finally surrendered after a brief but noisy wrestling bout.

Downstairs, everyone exchanged small gifts: books, sweaters, socks, pens, mints (for Matthew), bracelets, and the like. Everyone, that is, except Declan, who had no gifts to give anyone. Matthew and Kate made him a small regular allowance, but he was saving it for his return to Ireland. "I told you. I don't believe in Christmas. I want no gifts," he declared.

"Don't fuss yourself, Declan, love," said Kate. "The gifts are only small ones."

For an answer, Declan took himself out and down the cliff to the beach, where he sat alone on his usual rock and stared out to sea.

When he returned two hours later, they were all back from Mass. Kate and Matthew were both busy in the kitchen; Ana and Thomas acted as though nothing had happened. Mr. Sawchuk from the general store and another man had come back from Mass with them and sat talking in the living room, glasses of Matthew's homemade elderberry wine in their fists.

"What's Bent Benny doing here?" Declan asked Ana. Bent Benny was a familiar figure. Bent and crippled, he pushed his cart full of empty bottles and cans around the village. Some of the kids made fun of him.

"Matthew and Kate usually have him and Mr. Sawchuk over for Christmas dinner," said Ana.

There were seven of them around the kitchen table for dinner. Then Miss Ritter came downstairs wearing a blue dress and silver earrings and there were eight. Bent Benny's real name, Declan discovered, was Benjamin Oberman. Matthew and Kate called him Mr. Oberman.

They ate dinner and there was a lot of talk.

Matthew was unusually talkative. He said, "Christmas always reminds me of when I first met Kate."

"You met in Ireland, of course," said Miss Ritter.

"It was at a *ceilidh* – an Irish dance," said Kate, "a few days before Christmas."

"She was the prettiest girl there," said Matthew.

Kate smiled.

"It snowed that night," said Matthew gloomily, "and the snow was general all over Ireland."

Kate and Mr. Oberman laughed.

Declan recognized the famous line from James Joyce. It was the final line of *The Dead*. He remembered Miss Reardon, his literature teacher, explaining how snow had something to do with death, or the lack of love in the world, he couldn't remember exactly which. Right now he didn't care.

Mr. Sawchuk said, "When I was a young man in a logging camp up near Rupert, our Christmas dinner was eaten by a grizzly bear. It was a good dinner, like the one here today, roast turkey with all the trimmin's. The bear must have been woke up outta his hibernation by the noise of the trucks and the saws, and smelled the food and come barrelin' in just as we were all sittin' down to eat. We got outta there pretty fast, you bet. Then some of the men wanted to shoot it, but most thought it'd be a bad thing to go killin' on Christmas Day, so we let it alone and we waited until it'd gone away. We ended up eatin' pancakes 'n' syrup for Christmas dinner."

Everyone laughed.

▷ **1** *chill sb.:* make sb. cold **7** *burst:* enter energetically **10** *groan:* make a sound of disapproval **13** *surrender:* give up · *bout* [baʊt]: wrestling contest **17** *allowance:* amount of money given regularly **29** *elderberry:* Holunderbeere **45** *ceilidh* ['keɪli] **52** *James Joyce* (1882–1941): Irish writer **53** *The Dead:* last short story within the collection *Dubliners* by James Joyce **60** *trimmings:* extras, e.g. vegetables, at a Christmas meal · *hibernation:* deep sleep (of animals) during the winter

Mr. Oberman started to tell about a Christmas in a prisoner-of-war camp. Declan got up. "Excuse me," he said. He pushed back his chair and left the table and sat outside on the porch.

Kate came out and sat beside him. "Are you all right, Declan?"

"It's all the talk. Makes me restless, that's all."

They sat together in silence.

After a while, Declan said, "Go back in. I'm all right.'

Kate nodded. "You're just restless. You're all right."

"I think it's more than restless. I feel trapped here. You and Matthew and Ana and Thomas have me trapped. And Pender School and living here and all this Christmas stuff makes me feel like I'm in this huge steel cage like a ..." He clenched his fists.

Kate said nothing. She put her arm round his shoulder and gave it a squeeze.

Declan got up and walked down off the porch. Before he headed for the beach, he turned to Kate and said, "I'm out of the cage in a week, Kate, remember that!"

* * *

Later that evening, Declan, Ana, and Thomas were left alone with the last of the fire in the living room. It was late, almost time for bed. Matthew and Kate sat in their favorite spots in the family room-kitchen, talking and drinking tea.

Declan said, "I think I could guess why you ate none of the turkey, Ana."

"I'm sure you could. I saw you noticing. Ever since Harper, I think of how we eat other animals."

Declan gazed sleepily into the red centers of the burning logs.

"It's not as if we couldn't eat other things instead," said Ana.

"I like turkey and stuffing," said Thomas.

Ana laughed. "We know you do, Thomas. You had more than everyone else put together." She made a circle in front of her stomach with her hands and arms and made her eyes pop.

Thomas laughed.

Declan was still gazing into the fire. "What are you thinking about?" said Ana.

Declan made no reply.

"You're thinking about next week. About going back, aren't you!"

Declan nodded. “That’s right.” He was mesmerized by the fire.

“We were all praying you would stay. Prayers are not always answered.”

“You know I can’t stay.”

“You don’t care about us, do you?” Ana sounded angry.

Declan looked at her. “I do care about you. All of you.”

“Then why go back? You’re happy here.”

“You know why.”

“Will you go back to your old house?”

Declan shook his head. “Somebody else will have it now. The rent hasn’t been paid for months.”

“What about your things?”

He shrugged. “Mrs. O’Malley probably cleared everything out.”

“Then where will you go?”

“Matthew and Kate want me to go to Kate’s sister. She’s married and they have two kids. Her name is Bernadette McGuire. Lives in East Belfast, nice house and car.”

“Will you go there?”

“Maybe, maybe not. I can take care of myself. Mrs. O’Malley will give me a bed if I need one.”

Ana and Thomas went upstairs to bed. Declan threw another small alder log on the fire and sat watching it burn away to nothing.

▷ **37** *mesmerize sb.:* hold sb.’s attention completely

TWENTY THREE

The morning after Christmas day was gray and cold.

Declan slept late. When he got up, Kate was sitting in the kitchen alone reading a magazine, a cup of tea on the table beside her. "Ana and Thomas have gone into town to the indoor swimming pool," she said. "I didn't let them wake you. They waited for you until it was time for the nine-thirty bus. Make yourself some breakfast."

"I'm not hungry."

"Then help yourself to tea or juice."

Declan poured himself a cup of tea. "Where's Matthew?"

"Working. He's behind on his TV repairs. Maybe you could take him a mug of tea when you've finished your own."

Declan found him with his head in the back of a TV. "Kate sent tea."

Matthew heaved a sigh and put down his soldering iron. He took the tea. "Thanks."

Declan turned to go.

"Would you sit with me for a minute or two, Declan? There's something I need to tell you."

Declan sat up on the bench and waited while Matthew settled himself beside the electric heater with his tea.

"You'll soon be on your way back to Ireland."

Declan nodded. "That's right."

"You're still bent on leaving us, then?"

"Yes, Matthew, I am. That was the deal."

His uncle nodded thoughtfully and stirred his tea.

"About your return ticket."

Declan said nothing.

"I booked your flight for Tuesday the fifth. Midweek is cheaper. That okay?"

"That's fine." He waited. Then: "What do you want to tell me?"

"It's a terrible hard thing for me to talk about."

Declan waited.

"I want to tell you about Liam.

"My da? What about him?"

"I want to tell you about the time ..." Matthew paused and started again. "Liam was two years older than me. When he died, he was only thirty-five. That may seem old to you, but your da died a young man. He died the year your sister Mairead was born, leaving Mary, your ma, with a newborn baby and yourself, a three-year-old. It was 1981." Matthew paused and sipped his tea.

Declan said nothing, waiting for him to go on.

"Your da was a member of the Provos, the IRA. So was I."

"You? In the IRA? I don't believe it," Declan said with a sneer.

Matthew's face was tense. The hand holding the mug of tea trembled. "Well, you'd *better* believe it," he said, with a quiet, uncharacteristic force.

Declan watched his uncle for a few moments in silence, and then he said quietly, "I know about my da. He was IRA. My da was a hero. Shot by a gang of filthy Protestant militants. An Irish martyr."

"Your da was shot, that's right. But it wasn't the Protestants who shot him."

"Then it must have been the English!"

Matthew shook his head. "We were national liberation fighters. IRA! The Irish Republican Army! We were proud. Your da held rank: He was the second-in-command under the chief himself. Me? I was a nobody in the bomb squad." Matthew looked up at Declan as though waiting for him to make a sneering remark. When Declan said nothing, Matthew said, "The police found explosives and mercury tilt switches in a laundry hamper in the laundry room shared by several houses on your da's block. Nobody knows how they got there; I think

▷ **14** *soldering iron:* tool used to solder (= löten) things together **23** *bent on doing sth.:* determined to do sth. **25** *stir sth.:* move sth. (e.g. a liquid) with a spoon to mix it **40** *sip* (v): drink by only taking in very small amounts of a liquid **58** *mercury:* Quecksilber **58–59** *tilt switch:* Kippschalter **59** *laundry:* clothes or sheets that need washing or were washed · *hamper:* large basket

the police probably planted them. We'll never know. Your da and your ma were picked up for questioning – 'lifted' as we used to say."

"It's still lifted," said Declan quietly.

Matthew stared at the mug in his hand. "Your ma was pregnant with Mairead, and she was never the strong woman in those days. She suffered from headaches, and a weakness would come over her, and she'd have to lie down, and your da would feed her soup and talk to her. He was a good husband. He did the best he could.

"When your da and your ma were picked up by the police, your da begged them to let your poor mother go: she wasn't strong, she could suffer a miscarriage. You understand what I'm talking about, Declan?"

Declan nodded.

"But the police kept her. You were only three years old. Kate and I took care of you while your da and ma were in the police cells.

"After a couple of days, the police came in to your da in his cell and told him your mother had confessed about the explosives. She had done no such thing, of course, but Liam believed the lies the police told him, that she'd broken down under the questioning. He begged them again to let her go."

Matthew put down his mug on the bench. "The possession of explosives is an automatic life sentence in Ireland."

"I know."

"Your da knew for certain that the prison would kill your poor ma. And what about the baby? The police were ruthless. They would let her go on one condition, they said. Your da would work for the police. He would pass on information about IRA activities. The police would use the information to save lives. That's what they said. They would cover him. No one would be arrested. Your da agreed. He had no choice." Matthew stopped and looked into Declan's eyes. "Your da became an informer."

Declan felt the rage rise within him. He leaped off the bench. "You're a liar, Matthew! My father was no tout for the police! You're lying!" he snarled. "I don't believe any of it!"

"Listen to me, Declan. I'm telling you the God's truth, and when I'm finished you can believe what you like."

"What are you two talking about in there?" It was Ana and Thomas back from their swimming.

"Leave us be for five minutes!" shouted Matthew.

When they had gone, Matthew said, "Your da became a spy for the police. Nobody knew. Nobody guessed. He gave information about IRA attacks on the Brits, information about bombs, everything. He couldn't get out of it. If he stopped the flow of information, then the police would tell the IRA on him. And you know what that would mean: instant execution. The IRA always kills informers as a lesson to others, always. No informer goes free. So far up to then, they'd executed at least a dozen of their own men for informing on them." Matthew gave a bitter laugh. "They've shot many more since."

Declan could hardly hold still. He clenched his fists and clamped his jaw tight.

Matthew took his time. His voice was slow and deep. "The police kept their word at first. They arrested nobody. Then the IRA came up with a plan for a major hit on the British army. It was to be a big bomb. If everything went right, it would wipe out half a battalion. Liam was the only one who knew of the plan besides the IRA chief and the bomb squad, which included me. But the Brits were waiting for them. The bomb squad was stopped in the early hours of the morning, the bomb in their possession. Nobody escaped. The Brits should have arrested them – an automatic life sentence – but they didn't. They put the four men up against the truck and shot them.

"There was only one way the Brits could have known. Somebody had informed. But who? The IRA picked your da up for questioning. He confessed. They kept him three weeks. Then they shot him."

"That isn't true," said Declan through his teeth. "My father was killed by a gang of Protestant militants! You made it all up! I don't believe it! My father was never a traitor, I don't care what you say!"

"It was no dishonor! He did it out of love for your mother, Declan. But they tricked him. They swore they'd kill no one. 'It's to save lives,' they said. It was no dishonor to your da. They didn't keep their promises. If I had had a family, I'd have done exactly the same myself."

Declan was trying not to let Matthew see him cry, but he couldn't help himself. He wiped his eyes with the back of his hand. "And what were you doing in all of this, Matthew? Maybe it was yourself who

▷ **11** *miscarriage:* loss of a foetus before birth **22** *life sentence:* punishment of lifelong imprisonment **25** *ruthless:* showing no pity or mercy **26** *condition:* thing on which another thing depends **33** *tout* [taʊt] (sl): informer **54** *wipe sth. out:* destroy sth. completely **67** *dishonor* (NAmE) = (BE) *dishonour* (fml): loss of honour (= Ehre)

was the tout! Not my da. Didn't you just finish saying you were in the bomb squad? Then how was it they shot them all – four men – shot up against the truck you said – and you weren't there? How do you explain that, Matthew? Why weren't you there doing your job? How is it you're alive today if you were such a big liberation fighter?" Declan felt himself trembling.

Matthew shook his head sadly. "I was their first suspect, right enough. Your da saved my life, Declan, and that's the truth of it. He knew the bomb squad would be arrested and sent to jail for life – he never expected the Brits to kill, though – and he came to me on the morning of the hit with a job to do. I was to go to Derry with a package for the chief of operations there. It was urgent, he told me. I did as ordered – your da was the number-two man in Belfast, remember – and I delivered the package.

"When I returned to Belfast the next day, it was in the papers. Four IRA men found with a bomb and shot while trying to escape. That's what the papers said. The Brits lied: The squad never tried to escape; how could they? They were surrounded! Later, when the IRA picked up your da for informing, I knew. I knew it was my own brother who had saved me, sending me away to safety on a fool's errand. He wanted to save me from jail. He didn't know he was also saving my life. I knew then that he was the informer." Matthew looked at Declan. "I should have died that day with my squad."

Declan glared at his uncle. "You're alive today," he said between his teeth, "because my da died."

Matthew nodded. He sat forward, his elbows on his knees, staring at the garage floor. "After your sister was born, we left Ireland, Kate and I, that very same year Liam was shot. We'd had enough of it. I didn't want the same thing to happen to Kate that happened to your ma."

"You were the cowards! You ran to save yourselves! And you're making it all up about my da! He was no informer! He was no traitor! It's you who's the traitor, Matthew! You!"

Matthew stood up awkwardly. "In God's name, will you listen to me ..."

Declan tried to say more, but nothing would come out.

Matthew gripped Declan's arms in steel fingers. "They're both wrong, Declan, don't you see that? The IRA and the Protestants are both wrong! They're killing each other! What good does it do?

Violence isn't the answer! Don't go back there, Declan. Stay here with us. You'll never stop the madmen of the world from killing each other. You're not like them, Declan. You cannot go back to all that!"

Declan wrenched himself out of his uncle's grip and fled from the garage, burning with rage.

▷ **7** *suspect* ['- -] (n): person that is supposed to be guilty of a crime **12** *urgent:* needing immediate action **20** *errand:* short journey to deliver or get sth. (for sb.) **34** *awkward:* not graceful

TWENTY FOUR

Declan ran blindly.

He saw his uncle's truck, its keys dangling from the ignition, and he threw himself in and slammed the door. He pushed his foot down hard on the clutch and turned the key. The engine started. He pumped the accelerator. The engine stalled. In a black frenzy, he snatched at the choke knob and tried again. The engine roared to life. He looked out the window. Matthew was running toward him. His foot still on the clutch, Declan pushed the gearshift forward into first and let out the clutch too fast. The truck leaped forward, and he was away, taking part of the cedar hedge with him.

He twisted the wheel wildly, heading out onto the road that led to the ferry at Langdale, the back of the truck fishtailing out of control. He wrestled the wheel, trying to steady the truck's erratic flight, but only made things worse. The engine roared. The truck bucked and leaped away from him, over the road and into the ditch, nose first, and came to a sudden and complete stop with its back in the air.

He sat stunned by the impact, chest jammed tight against the wheel.

The next thing he knew, his uncle was pulling him out of the truck and dragging him up out of the ditch and onto the side of the road. He struggled against Matthew's grip. "I'm all right. Let me go!"

He straightened up.

"Are you hurt?"

"I told you. I'm all right."

He looked at the truck angled down into the ditch, its nose submerged under two feet of water, its tailgate lifted high in the air. It would need a tow truck and a winch to pull it out.

He limped to the house and up the stairs to his room. The door had no lock, so he closed it and wedged the back of a chair under the knob so no one could get in.

After awhile, Kate came up and knocked on the door.

"Go away," he said.

She tried the door. It remained firmly shut.

"Are you all right, Declan? Let me in a minute."

"Go away."

She went.

A few minutes later, Ana knocked. "Declan, let me talk to you, please!"

"Go away!"

They left him alone until dinnertime. Kate knocked on the door. He pretended to be asleep. "Declan, will you come down for your dinner before it goes cold?"

Silence.

"Then I'll bring up a bite of your favorite – mince pie and fresh cream."

"Leave me alone!"

"Declan?"

"Leave me alone!"

She went away and left him alone.

He stayed there for the rest of the day, lying on his bed, his eyes closed against the pain in his heart, thinking over and over again about what Matthew had told him. "Listen to me, Declan!" Matthew's voice: "Listen to me, Declan!

"The IRA murdered your da.

"Your da was an informer, a tout.

"Listen to me!"

Declan imagined the execution: his da with his hands tied behind his back, a bag over his head, the IRA executioner shooting him in the

▷ **4** *clutch:* Kupplung **5** *stall:* stop suddenly because of insufficient power or speed **13** *erratic:* irregular **15** *ditch:* Graben **17** *stunned:* shocked **26** *submerge:* go under the surface of water · *tailgate:* door at the back of a car or lorry **27** *tow truck* (NAmE): truck that can pull another vehicle with a rope · *winch:* Winde **28** *limp* (v): walk unevenly

back of the head – Declan knew how it was done, he had heard the stories of IRA justice. Just one shot; that was all it took, they said. His da. Shot in the head. An informer ("Listen to me, Declan!"), a traitor to the Irish cause.

"Listen to me, Declan! Listen to me! I'm telling you the God's truth!" Matthew defending his brother: "Liam Doyle put love for his wife and family first, before Ireland's struggle for freedom. So they killed him, a man with a pregnant wife. You've got to listen to me, Declan!"

Matthew had told him all this, and Declan believed it. He had to believe it. Why would Matthew lie?

But what was it he had said about the fighting? "They're both wrong, Declan, don't you see that? The IRA and the Protestants are both wrong! They're killing each other! What good does it do?"

Was he to believe his uncle Matthew that his da's death had been all in vain, that they were all wrong? All wasting lives? That their fight for what was rightfully theirs was achieving nothing but more and more hatred and unending violence? The Holy Terrors, too? Wrong?

After a long time, he fell asleep.

When he woke up, it was dark, with a moon. He got off the bed and sat staring out the window at the black rocks and the ocean.

* * *

He came down to breakfast the next morning, his eyes puffy.

Kate touched Declan's shoulder. He wriggled away. "Ah, you must be destroyed with the hunger. Sit down and I'll make you some pancakes." She pushed the jug of orange juice across the table toward him.

Matthew was sitting in his usual chair, reading a thick book. He looked up anxiously and nodded and went back to his book.

Declan poured himself a glass of juice. He looked at his uncle. "Sorry about the truck."

Matthew raised his head. "The truck can be fixed. It was yourself we were worried about."

"I'm okay."

Matthew nodded again.

Father O'Connor poked his head in the back door. "God save all here!"

"Come in, Father, I've tea made," said Kate.

"You're the hard-working woman, Katherine," said the priest, smiling, and sitting down at the table. "Matthew," he said to Matthew.

Matthew nodded. "Mornin', Father." He put aside his book.

Ana came down the stairs, her face dark with temper. "I'm fed up with him! He can go ..."

"What ails you, girl?" said Kate. "Say good morning to Father O'Connor."

"Morning, Father." Ana rolled her eyes to the ceiling. "Thomas is acting up. He wants to wear a shirt with buttons instead of a T-shirt. Don't ask me why. He got the buttons fastened all wrong, and when I tried to fix them, he pushed me away and started yelling and carrying on. And he says he won't come down to breakfast; he wants to stay in his room like ..." She looked at Declan and stopped.

"Sit down, Ana, and don't bother your head about the boy," said Kate. "Sometimes it's best to leave him be. Buttons is only buttons."

Father O'Connor sipped his tea.

Thomas, on the top landing, leaned his head over the banister rail. "Piss! Piss! Piss!" he screamed.

Father O'Connor's cup rattled against the saucer.

* * *

It snowed on New Year's Eve, starting in the morning and falling thickly. In the afternoon, they built a snowman, which Thomas said looked like Matthew because it was so big.

They stayed up late with the radio turned to CBC and toasted the new year at midnight with some of Matthew's elderberry wine.

Kate said, "May the good Lord and all His holy saints and angels make the new year a happy one for us all!"

The next morning it snowed again. Ana and Thomas tobogganed, using sheets of cardboard. Declan watched them for awhile as they screamed and tumbled. Ana begged him to join in, but he shook his head and went off alone in the snow.

▷ **16** *in vain:* useless · *waste sth.:* do sth. which has no reason **22** *puffy:* thick and swollen **25** *jug* (BE) = (NAmE) *pitcher:* deep container for liquids **41** *temper:* (here) anger **54** *banister rail:* Geländerbrüstung **64** *toboggan* [tə'bɒgən] (v): slide down a snowy hill on a sledge

All was white and new. New year. New snow. He took the buried path leading along the cliff, between the sea and the mountain, the snow in his hair and eyes. The going was slow. He did not walk far, just far enough to be alone, away from the house, away from people. He stood with his hands thrust deep into his jacket pockets, listening to the ocean and watching the gulls, their cries muffled by the snow. He turned and scanned the high, snowy trees of the forest, breathing in the cold clean air and the silence and peace of this land, so far and so different from his own.

His own land. His own people. His own family dead. Wasted lives. He felt with his thumb the gold ring on his finger and remembered the plain gravestone with its three names in Milltown Cemetery. They were dead and he was alive and it was a new year.

He watched the snow piling up on the branches of the trees, bending them lower and lower with its weight. When it seemed that the overladen branches were about to snap, they sprang suddenly back, catapulting showers of powdered snow into the air.

He turned. The ocean stretched out in front of him, flat and glimmering under a leaden sky. He stood in the cold brightness of the snow and felt the vast quiet of the land melting into him.

TWENTY FIVE

This was the day.

Declan had hardly slept. He sat on the edge of his bed and stared out the window at the darkness.

The house was quiet.

He was trying not to think. Thinking only made things worse. "Don't think," he told himself. "Do what you have to do, but don't think."

The sky was growing lighter; he could see the ocean now and the black rocks. He did not think. He breathed. He sat. He opened the window wider and shivered with the cold. Smell of the sea. Creak of the house. Someone was up. Light footsteps at his door. Faint knock.

"Can I come in?" Ana whispering through the gloom. She came to him. "I couldn't sleep." She was dressed; jeans and T-shirt. She sat beside him on the edge of his rumpled bed. "You couldn't sleep either, looks like."

"I slept," lied Declan. He stood. He wore only Jockey shorts to bed. He pulled open the drawer of the chest and took out a clean T-shirt and shrugged himself into it. His jeans were on the top of the chest, where he had left them last night. He pulled them on. No thinking allowed. Socks, bottom drawer. He sat on the bed beside Ana and pulled them on.

"I kept thinking of you going away from us," said Ana. Declan said nothing.

▷ **16** *snap:* break suddenly **30** *creak* (n): Knarren **34** *rumple sth.:* make sth (esp. a bed) untidy

"I thought of you flying in the airplane back to Ireland. Alone. Nobody meeting you when you get there ..."

"I told you ..."

"I know. But nobody who knows and cares about you." Declan slipped his feet into his sneakers.

"We care about you."

He tied the laces of his sneakers. Don't think. He began throwing his few things into his bag. T-shirts ...

"You don't care about us, do you, Declan?"

... shorts, socks ...

"You won't miss us."

"Of course I'll miss you." He stopped packing and looked at her. "All of you. I wish I could stay."

"So stay."

He turned away. "We've been through this stuff, Ana. I can't stay." He was trying not to think, but she was making it very difficult for him. "You know I have to go home. It's where my family is buried." He finished his packing and dropped the small bag on the floor near the door.

Ana stood, took two small steps to the window, and looked out. "But this is your home. We're your family now. I want you to stay."

He stood beside her at the window. The sky was brighter now; he could see the beach below the cliff. "Harper wanted to stay, too, remember?"

Ana nodded.

"But he finally had to go home to the sea," said Declan.

"The sea was the only home Harper really had," said Ana.

"But he left, didn't he? He had to go; he couldn't stay!"

Ana gave a snort of disgust. "You're not a seal, Declan! You're a person! What you need is here, not in ..."

There was a tap on the door. Matthew poked his head in. "Come down for breakfast. We have to leave in under an Wake Thomas, will you, Ana?"

Ana left. Declan wanted no breakfast. He waited until it was late and then he went downstairs.

Kate handed him a glass of juice. "It's not too late to change your mind, Declan, love. We don't want you to go, we're destroyed with the thought of it, so we are, isn't that right, Matthew?"

Matthew nodded mournfully.

Declan shook his head.

Matthew climbed behind the wheel of Mr. Sawchuk's scarred old Chevrolet Biscayne. Kate sat beside him. Matthew's truck was still out of action; Mr. Sawchuk had insisted they use his car. "Got good snow tires," he had said. "Might as well use her."

Declan sat in the back with Ana and Thomas. Though there had been no new snow, the drive to Langdale took close to an hour.

Declan said nothing the whole way.

They drove onto the ferry. Matthew and Kate stayed in the car for the short trip to Horseshoe Bay, but Declan, Ana, and Thomas climbed out and wandered around the ferry deck. Ana and Thomas had very little to say; Thomas was unusually quiet. Declan stood at the rail staring down at the oil-green water sliding past the hull of the ferryboat.

They drove off the ferry at Horseshoe Bay. Nobody spoke much on the drive to the airport. Kate, who always had something to say, was almost silent. She sat with her eyes to the front.

The snow in Vancouver had been cleared from the main roads. By the time they reached the airport, the sun was shining weakly.

Declan had no suitcase to check in, only his carry-on bag stuffed with clothing and his map of British Columbia, which Matthew had said he could keep.

Matthew gave him his passport and his flight tickets and explained again the route and the timing: Vancouver to Prestwick, Scotland; a two-hour wait; then Prestwick to Belfast. He would be met at Belfast airport by Kate's sister, Bernadette.

"It's still not too late to change your mind," said Kate. "You can still come back with us. We love you, Declan, all of us. We want you to stay. It sickens the heart out of us all to see you leaving."

Declan shook his head. He did not speak.

Kate gave a deep sigh. "Keep your tickets in your passport. You'll need the boarding pass, so keep that separate. I've written down Bernadette's telephone number and her address in your passport in case something goes wrong and she's late to pick you up. Also our address and telephone at Otter Harbour." She kissed him on the cheek. "I put a few candies in your bag for something to chew on, and a sandwich in case you get hungry. Matthew put in a couple of

▷ **52** *hull:* body of a ship **75** *candy* (n) (NAmE): sweet

paperbacks for you to read. Ah! God go with you, Declan." She kissed him again, then turned away.

Matthew's eyes were wet. He stuck out his hand. Declan shook it.

"Good-bye, Declan," said Ana. She kissed him quickly on the cheek and stood back and held Thomas by the hand. She was wearing her big sunglasses.

Thomas began to make grunting noises. "Aagh! Agh!" he cried. He pulled away from Ana and, arms out-stretched, lunged at Declan, but tripped and fell clumsily at his feet. He gripped Declan's ankles and hung on as though by sheer strength he would prevent him from moving away. "Don't go, Declan!" he cried.

Declan crouched down and pulled Thomas's arms away from his ankles. "Take it easy, Thomas." He helped him up. "Take it easy."

Declan turned and walked through gate number eight, his bag slung over his shoulder. He brushed the hair out of his eyes. Just before he turned the corner out of sight, he saw them standing together. He waved to them. They waved back. He headed into the waiting room and sat down with his bag on his knees. He could see the Canadian Airways 747 airplane through the window.

He did not have to wait long. He handed his boarding pass to the uniformed woman at the tunnel that led to the airplane. She wore bright red lipstick.

His seat was more than halfway down the aisle. There was already someone in the outside seat, a heavy man in a business suit. Declan opened the luggage compartment over the man's head, pushed his bag in, and slammed it shut. "Excuse me," he muttered. The man clutched his briefcase in balloon fingers and struggled to his feet. Declan slid past him to the window seat and fastened the seat belt around his middle. He pressed his forehead against the window and saw the jet engines that soon would be above the clouds, flying him home.

He had managed to stop thinking all morning, but now as he looked out the plane window, thoughts began to trickle through, the way water does before a dam bursts. He could not stop them coming, so he concentrated on thoughts of home. They would be surprised in Belfast to see him back. The O'Malleys. Brendan Fogarty's surprised face. This time he was really going home. So why wasn't he excited?

He looked out at the snow-capped mountains. He would miss all this, the vast, peaceful, forested land, and the sea, and the sharp air that smelled of cedar and pine and mountain alder.

He thought of Harper swimming out to sea on his way home, and he remembered the way he had felt, that sense of loss, watching the seal's black shiny nose and bristled whiskers heading away from him.

And he felt again that deadly emptiness and despair he'd felt before when he had sat alone on his bed in his and Mairead's room under the Sacred Heart picture, knowing with an awful certainty he would never see his sister or his ma ever again.

He leaned back on the headrest and closed his eyes, remembering, the memories coming to him in fragments:

Joe's slow smile. The joy on his face after running the canoe through the white-water needle. Declan remembers Matthew's face as he holds out his hand. "Mint?" Matthew bending over a TV set, his big hands resting, limp on his knees, as he searches with his eyes through the mass of colored circuits and transistors before picking up his soldering iron. Matthew carrying in his arms a sick seal up the steep cliff. Matthew watching a cougar along the sights of his rifle, hoping it will run to safety. Declan remembers Kate, sitting tall on the edge of a rock, catching the shades and colors of the sea and the sky, her lips tight with concentration as she follows the play of light and shadow. Kate, pouring Declan a glass of orange juice from a plastic pitcher. Kate, listening to Ana blathering on at her about her schoolwork, or an animal she saw, or what she said to Leah, or how she is fed up with Thomas not doing as he is told. Ana, singing softly to herself a song she had been rehearsing. Ana's green eyes flashing with fury at Declan when he killed the squirrel. Ana fixing Thomas's sweater, bunched at the shoulders, or running to grab Thomas's arm, afraid he'll run out into the road under the school bus. And he remembers Thomas, happy as he shows Declan a pair of oak bookends he made at school and wanting Declan to have them to keep tidy the small pile of books Declan has amassed on his chest of drawers.

▷ **10** *sheer:* complete **26** *mutter:* murmur **33** *trickle:* come slowly **39** *vast* [væst; BE vɑːst]: large in area **53** *limp* (adj): not stiff **54** *circuit:* Schaltkreis **56** *steep:* rising or falling sharply **61** *blather* (infml): talk continuously **65** *fury:* wild anger **68** *oak:* Eiche **69** *bookend:* support to keep books upright **70** *amass sth.:* collect sth. in large quantities

"You all right, boy?" said the man beside him.

Declan looked at him. Of course he was all right. Why shouldn't he be all right? The man blurred. Then Declan realized his eyes were wet.

He clawed at the buckle of his seat belt. "Excuse me." He pushed past the man into the aisle, jerked open the luggage compartment, snatched his bag, and ran to the airplane door.

"What!" The flight attendant threw up her hands in astonishment as Declan flew by her.

He ran up the rubber-matted slope of the tunnel into the waiting room. The baggage examiners had gone; the X-ray equipment was deserted. He dashed through the barrier and burst into the terminal.

They had gone.

Perhaps they were up in the lounge watching for the airplane to take off. Or they could still be in the parking lot. He ran out of the terminal, down the steps, and across the road to the parking lot.

Where had Matthew parked the car? It was such a huge lot: row after row of cars. Declan had seen nothing on the way in. Only the Hertz car-rental sign. That was the row.

He ran along the row checking the cars. Finally! There! The scarred blue Biscayne! There was no mistaking the old car. No sign of them. He put his bag on the car roof and sat on the trunk. He watched and waited.

The Canadian Airlines 747 arrowed up into the clouds.

Without him.

One empty seat.

He did not have to wait long after that. He saw them in the distance, the four of them, walking toward the car-rental sign at the beginning of the row. They came slowly. They had not seen him.

He sat waiting for them.

▷ **3** *blur:* become unclear **5** *claw at sb./ sth.:* scratch or tear at sb./sth. with one's fingernails · *buckle:* Schnalle **12** *dash:* rush

James Heneghan was born in 1930. He grew up in Liverpool and Belfast. He went to the De La Salle Grammar School in Liverpool after which he joined the Royal Air Force from 1949–1951. After that he worked as a shipping clerk and a policeman.

In 1957 he emigrated to Canada and settled in British Columbia where he continued working with the police, being a fingerprint technician for the Vancouver Police for the following 12 years. At the age of 39 he enrolled at Simon Fraser University in Burnaby, B.C., where he obtained his BA in English and Political Science and then became an English teacher in the Burnaby School District for the next 20 years – until he retired.

Apparently life as a pensioner did not seem quite what he would have been satisfied with. When asked the reason for becoming an author, he once quite unpretentiously answered: "I retired from teaching and needed something to do; it was either writing, golf, cross-country running, training for an Olympic gold in underwater hockey, I chose writing. Besides I needed the money."

Before *Torn Away*, he published *Puffin Rock* (1980), *Goodbye, Carleton High* (1983), *Blue* (1992), a story about a boy and his dog, which is his personal favourite, and *Wish Me Luck* (1997), which is his most autobiographical novel to date.

With his wife Lucy, James Heneghan presently lives in Vancouver. He has four grown up children.